POETRY
Rivals 2015

✩✩✩✩✩✩✩✩✩✩✩

THE FINALISTS

✩✩✩✩✩✩✩✩✩✩✩

EDITED BY
JENNI BANNISTER

First published in Great Britain in 2016 by:
Forward Poetry
Remus House
Coltsfoot Drive
Peterborough
PE2 9BF
Telephone: 01733 890099
Website: www.forwardpoetry.co.uk

All Rights Reserved
Book Design by Spencer Hart
© Copyright Contributors 2015
SB ISBN 978-1-84418-706-5

Printed and bound in the UK by BookPrintingUK
Website: www.bookprintinguk.com

FOREWORD

In 2009, Poetry Rivals was launched. It was one of the biggest and most prestigious competitions ever held by Forward Poetry. Due to the popularity and success of this talent contest like no other, we have taken Poetry Rivals into 2015, where it has proven to be even bigger and better than last year.

Poets of all ages and from all corners of the globe were invited to write a poem that showed true creative talent - a poem that would stand out from the rest. All of the entries were assessed by the Poetry Rivals editors and judge Mark Grist, who then picked the top 100 poets. From these a shortlist of 30 finalists has been chosen to go on to perform at the Poetry Rivals Slam Final, where a panel of expert judges will select a winner who will be awarded 1st prize of a pamphlet publishing contract with Burning Eye Books.

This anthology brings the poems of the longlisted poets together in an inspiring collection of verse. Reflecting the vibrancy of the modern poetic world, it is brimming with imagination and diversity.

As well as encouraging creative expression, Poetry Rivals has also given writers a vital opportunity to showcase their work to the public, thus providing it with the wider audience it so richly deserves.

CONTENTS

THE POEMS

BEWARE OF THE TROLLS

They like to jab a needle in a touchy space,
An online provocation right against your face,
They seek your darkest corners and invade your souls,
They are nasty, worm-like phantoms, called the internet trolls

They post a ghastly picture, then they disappear,
Swamp your page with troubles and invade your fear,
They tunnel under virtual ground, sneaky Facebook moles,
They are shadows in your backyard, called the internet trolls

They gather several emails so they can change their name,
This lets them work in secret, they can hide their shame,
You'll hardly ever spot them, as they chase their goals,
They are damaged, friendless beings, called the internet trolls.

So children, in your nightmares, filled with thoughts you dread,
Be grateful for the monsters underneath your bed,
They will teach you self-protection and will keep you whole,
For the time you meet a demon, called the internet troll.

CLAIRE BALDRY

POETRY IS A BAD WORD

People say you shouldn't say poetry,
they say poetry is a bad word.
The typical implication is that
enjoyment in rhapsody means
employment's a mystery and yeah
I might be lacking
in that type of particular history
but I think that's why it's a risk to say poetry.
Especially in an interview situation,
'cause Cameron's nation's no place for creation
they'd ask me of my work ethic
and I'd say prophetic, but they'd just think I'm pathetic,
a bit of a dick, with an oversized thesaurus,
well can you not tell I'm sick
of it.
Poetry's not some public school flash in the pan nonsense,
chatting, 'Do you not think that he saw us
spray-painting cynical haikus
on Westminster's walls?'
No of course not, they'd cleaned it
by morning 'cause Cameron abhors us.
Poetry doesn't matter when it's not for the masses
a chance to say nonsense to those who oppress us,

but, I can play the part of the bad word poet,
if that's more appropriate,
overtly offensive, sexually frustrated
and more often than not vastly misinterpreted
and justly agitated, I don't care if you hate it,
'cause, don't you see I've had it with this duck-faced madness,
I refuse to say lyrical ballad
when defining my wordular trip hazards,
tripping up tongues I'm like Lennon on acid
baby yeah that's right, I'm not afraid to say it!
I'm just a bad poet, and what's worse is, I know it.
I've got bees' knees-like similes,
contemporary allegories,

marginally offensive half-witted ironies
and I'm only half sure that I know what they mean.
Yeah you might have a good job but
with my rhymes I be schooling you
rapping you up inside a rhapsodic hula hoop
popping you senseless, I don't care if I'm rude to you
this poet's just an egotist you handed a microphone.
And yeah you might be a doctor,
but just try and out-Seuss me,
oh the places you'll go when I ask you to show me
anything I think is better than a Year 2 essay.
Go sink your implications in a wishing well,
I bleed ink, can you not yet tell
you think my aspirations aren't right go to Hell
'cause poetry is the best game for getting laid,
baby, I can turn this thing around so it's just about mating,
ladies I'm a bad poet, and I know that you love it.

However, I want to say something that means something,
not just a lightly simmered revolutionary ideal
a real idea of how people really feel
when they're starving from taxes
and can't afford a meal,
when fat cat clap trap
tells us we're worthless
if you're poor it's on purpose
if you didn't go to Eton
they couldn't care less
it drives me to madness,
that satire is just reality.
So write yourself senseless if it helps you to cope
or if you know that it's pointless just line up the dope
but either way never let them tell you
that poetry is a bad word.

PATRICK CLARKE

3

TARANTISM

*(n. A nervous disorder characterised
by an uncontrollable impulse to dance)*

One, two, it's all up to you.
The tune takes over. Put on your shoes,
get on your feet, and dance before it's over.
Rapid, ecstatic, melodically moving along. The song
is strangely seductive, calls like a siren
higher and higher and higher. The fire
is irresistibly hot. You cannot
quench the frantic pyre,
want to or not.

Go on.
Embrace the heat.
Embrace the beat. The battle's won.
Make other people meet and greet with:
'They went dancing whirlwinds down the street.'

No.
No.
No, no, no, no.
It won't do,
It won't do, I tell you
for you to sit around,
not making your feet hit the ground
and not having your shoe
ta-tap the be-beat of the sound.
Get up! Move around!
Stop being so blue!
And dance!
Dance!
Dance!

Dance with your lover. Dance with your friend.
Dance with your mother. Dance with your pen.
Dance with a Barbie. Dance with a Ken.
Dance with another. Dance it again.
And again and again and again.
Dance through the summer.
Dance to the end.

One, two, nothing to do.
You have to keep up with the rhythm and it
just keeps on going faster, faster, faster.
The simple truth is that music is master
of soul and body. And no disaster
can break your dancing spirit
till she stops.

LARS MALMQVIST

ON SITTING NEXT TO JOHN COOPER-CLARKE ON A TRAIN

Evidently it's Cooper-Clarke – I'd know him even in the dark but
to say 'Hi John' seems too familiar – a wink would just be weird.
A nod? A continental kiss? I doubt that he would welcome this,
for he might be sick of sycophantic puppets.
He might think – *Go away – you muppet*
and please don't show me that crumpled verse
that you've probably got tucked away in your purse.
Even if I don't pose an immediate danger,
to him I am just a total stranger.

So I say nothing.
But it's hard.
Because at times when life has been truly shit
I've reached for his volumes of Salford grit.
So I want to say –
You're the punk Pied Piper.
You're a syllable sniper.
You're a slick soothsayer – you're a jargon slayer.
You're a peptic collector of sceptic wit.
A louche lounge lizard with a lot of lip.
You're a scene shape-shifter with an urban vista.
A true grit, drop kick comeback mister.
You're a verbal viper – you're a mean narrator.
You're my favourite social commentator.
You're my Shelley, Keats and Clare.
You've had more hits than Baudelaire!

But I say nothing for the entire journey
and on arrival at Manchester Piccadilly we both leave the train
and I rush ahead to find a doorway to smoke in.
A stick-thin figure joins me there – a man I would know anywhere and
in slanting rain and wind that whips we struggle with Rizlas and filter tips.
Then when he lights up John turns to say – he turns to say –
'Blooming smoking ban, eh!'
And I say, 'Yeah – right!'

If I said a lengthy chat ensued then that would be a fiction
but we shared the camaraderie of nicotine addiction
and only when we'd gone our separate ways
I realised what I really wanted to say and it was just –
Thank you – Thank you kindly Cooper-Clarke
poet, raconteur and clown,
rhythmic ranter, king of banter, metaphor and noun.
Thank you kindly Cooper-Clarke, for me you wear the crown.
You walked us down to Beasley Street
and you showed us Chicken Town.

MARY DICKINS

DESTROYER OF WORLDS

*(Based On The Atomic Bombings Of Hiroshima
And Nagasaki During WWII)*

A letter from a German god,
Did bring new players to the game;
Their moral thoughts we now think odd,
And nothing now would be the same.

Dreamt up by thinkers in their labs,
As a new way to kill and maim;
No one to question, or keep tabs,
And nothing now would be the same.

A naval base named for a jewel,
Presented a chance to proclaim:
That keeping this war on was cruel,
And nothing now would be the same.

Enola Gay took to the skies,
With Bockscar also taking aim;
Their cargo bore the stench of lies,
And nothing now would be the same.

When Little Boy and Fat Man fell,
Their death came like autumnal rain;
But hotter than the depths of hell,
And nothing now would be the same.

Now I have become death, he said,
As Oppenheimer took the blame;
Three hundred thousand people dead,
And nothing now would be the same.

As shadows burnt into the road,
Manhattan bowed its head in shame;
Whilst the new face of war had showed,
And nothing now would be the same.

Hiroshima was first to fall,
Then Nagasaki felt the flame;
As death encompassed one and all,
And nothing now would be the same.

But history fell like a veil,
So now children will read their name
As nothing more than a detail,
And nothing now would be the same.

SAM ILLINGWORTH

BURN AFTER READING

We smuggle doggy bags and house red,

Flash accents like wristbands; we're storm chasers
For a front row microphone splash zone
Where lightening, black as clouds across a sky of eyes rumbles.
Adrenaline raptured our thunderous hearts into applause.
There was a queue for the poetry tonight.

The city whispered across the Manx sea
And familiar pilgrimage
Struck me impatient as an emigrant.
So I've packed a shroud of silence
For a comeback revamp new look
Like you'd have to pay me to speak
But instead it's for listening.

See I'm pre-compost,
Waiting to be watered into an archipelago of bits and bones
From seeds skimmed like stones.
Roots grew, set, met and
Weakened me into strength.

I wake like flat cider,
Digging for cigarettes in dreams of old Saturdays.
I'd forgotten how to burn the curriculum,
Remembered only the tornado of two-steps
Smashing empties by the bar.

And all the books have barcodes now
Even the gentry've been left to homelessness
Since pews are not for sleeping.
Never you mind the length of them
Or now how empty.

Mercy's new war
Marches like snowploughs for the fallen.
Melting to the river named after the life in it;
The wasted, lost and washed ashore.

Ironic as Che Geuvara tee shirts,
We slam about gentrification
With Starbucks cups hanging off our lips;
Moaning holes in socks,
Holes in pockets
How pockets are just holes for money to pass through.
Whilst we're about one Zumba class away from bankrupting ourselves
on privilege
Show of hands –
How many poets do we have in the room?

There's no wine left in Dublin,
Not since dawn broke
And the scratch cards revealed American flags.
When 4th of July fireworks bang
We'll be the Fawkes shadows,
Burning books like it were the same thing
But the best flint for us is bone.
Bones in the Bataclan.
Bones on Turkish shores.
Bones to microphones,
So we just stand there
Melting.

An ex suggest pitching tents on stage
So the city sleepers can cook marshmallows,
But the chips we've stripped from shoulders
Burn the memories of kissing in graveyards
Illuminating how our grudges are just heirlooms.

We never wanted to be witness,
But we burn after reading
This is just smoke.
This is all just smoke

Of someone else's fire.

CIARÁN HODGERS

MY PLACE

I know it well, this place.
It's a safe place.
A private place.
A place to hide.
A place to play.
A place to form and fix things.
I can hold my dad's hand.
See his brown eyes.
Say the things I thought here but didn't say.
I can smell my newborn baby.
Hold a tiny foot in my hand.
Dance to the Smiths in a more eloquent way than I really did.
Or can.
Or would.
Wear pink eyeshadow.
Wear lace party tights.
Make a daisy chain under a tree long gone.
Cloud watch under a tree long gone.
Hold hands under a tree long gone.
Watch Tom and Jerry with new eyes.
Swim in the Indian Ocean.
Throw a sycamore seed.
Smell the soil after rain.
Watch a spider make a web.
Weave my future.
Their future.
Our future.
Gran's soup with barley.
The Beatles on the colour TV
Strawberry lip gloss.
My first kiss.
My last kiss.
My next kiss
An imagined day.
A lost day.
A hoped for day.
Have that conversation I should have had.

Have that conversation I didn't want.
Have that conversation with you.
Cry.
Giggle.
Worry.
Too much worry.
Insurmountable 4am problems.
What would I do if?
What would happen if?
Are they hurting?
Are they right?
Can I help?
Can I say?
Should I go?
Should I wait?
Will I manage?
Will I do?
It's always there.
No switch.
It's mine.
Different to yours and theirs.
His and hers.
It has no end that I can see.
Stores things I can't let go.
Stores things I can't recall.
Stores things I don't want.
Or need.
But makes me, me!
Audrey.
The girl who wonders and wanders.
And sews its new seeds.

AUDREY BISCOTTI

MIXED BLOOD

I was born in the land where selkies dwell
where the sea crashes endlessly
where the wind, rain and clouds collide in melodies
where mountains remind you quietly
of your size with their sincerity
and lochs contain depths of history
in cold waters only monsters breathe

I carry Celtic silver knotted about my wrist
for eternity
serpents consume one another
never finished – tongues on my arteries

but on my right are eight jade turtles
infinity on its side
immortalised in stone
green good fortune
I'm lucky I know
to have them with me
but so often their bodies weigh too heavy

so often
these bracelets and bangles transform into manacles
one silver, one stone
both claiming me as one of their own
pulling me apart, from east to west
west to east
my heart pumps a blend of whisky, blood and
boiling tea
as my body floats in the no-man's-land of sea
no land for me
but labels I get
endlessly
white masks reflecting my face
coloured with the cast of their prejudices onto me
grasping hands applying words
spiderwebs of assumptions
such fine silk but so sticky

words I never wanted
about worlds I've only ever haunted
unusual, exotic
you can't be Scottish
black ink scrawled across my skin
but only unfamiliar handwriting
this doesn't belong to me
what are you?
let me be

so I fight back with letters I engrave on my limbs
take a knife and let the blood fill them in
red for luck and joy
red like the lion
protecting the home I grew up in
roaring my heritage
a whole pride
a whole person
hardened under scrutinisation
sharpened to a succinct answer
to slice off these woven nets you tied me up in

but as my mouth is tearing at your knots, throttling
of *what are you*
let me scratch names upon your proud forehead, raised chin
let me brand you
with the white heat of British iron
I realise I'm free of you but not your words
for now my net is bigger and beautiful
more complex than one I've ever been caught in
fought in
but still I'm encased in definite definitions
solid cursive letters snagged on each other
hanging heavy round my throat
tangled and the more I say the more
I'm trapped

so I let go, become mist
amorphous
let silver and jade melt, evaporate
absorbed into me

absolving me of weight and obligation
I am constantly changing, shifting now
you can throw words now
and, sharp as they are
from years against the whetstone of
stereotypes
racism
misogyny
they will fly on through me
I do not have the language to encompass
my range of being
but I'm happy
to confuse you with my contentedness
in ambiguity
and my heart will continue to
pump a blend of whisky, blood and boiling tea
as my body floats in the no-man's-land of sea
no land for me
I own no land and no land owns me
flexible, in flux

adaptable and powerful
home is wherever I will be
and nothing you can say will take that from
within me
this is my ethnicity, identity
ever-changing and known and owned only
and forever
by me.

AILSA FINERON

THE CIRCLE

I see the sunny days.
The sober managers of building societies,
banks, maybe. Button bright
in their certain trajectories.

I see the neat wives, shining.

Millponds of virgin tarmac
hold back trees, allowing
the long hours to hide
small dramas like bones
in lawn-tidy gardens.

I see the blue sky corners.

Postboxes, hungry for gossip,
are gateway and godsend here.
Their slow digestion filling
these avenues with promise
for days, weeks maybe,
until response confirms the circle.

I see the sunny days
in ages tailed back on broken roads;
in the weed-full remnants of dead factories;
and in social media I feel I can't ignore.

TONY NOON

HAIRCUT

In the last few months
she started to cut her husband's hair
when the mob in his blood had lynched his health
and sentenced his body to stop.
The nurses
they thought they did a better job because
from time to time she would miss a little spot.
They'd tell her
put down the scissors
we do this a lot.
But she would snap her scissors
and cut a line through the air
which they were not to cross –
only she cut his hair.

So one day I asked her,
Why not let someone else have a try?
Why not take him to the salon
get your nails done in the meantime?

She said,
What's wrong with my nails?

Nothing!
But why must you alone cut his hair?

And she told me,
Because.

'Because I can't do a lot.
I can't bring down that thing that burdens him.
That unfair thing
that multiplies beneath his own skin
that dictates what he can eat
and say
and remember.
I can't un-plaster the propaganda
from his veins.
That fascist thing
that weighs down his limbs.

I would if I could but I can't
bring it to its knees as it has done him
push it out to sea as it has done him.
I would if I could but I can't keep him from sinking.
I've tried
for so long now.
I read all the right books
cooked all the right meals.
I gave him the pills and the lifejackets
the morphine patches
the prayers.
I mayday called the doctor a fool
when she told us this was it.
That books and food were of no use now
looking me down like I was lost
at sea.
But I am not.
And he is not.
He is not a ship.
He is not a metaphor.
He is a man who promised himself grey to me.
He promised me white hair
and wrinkles
and arthritis for God's sake.
Promised me Sunday mornings
talking over papers about the things we'd done
the children we'd raised
how the country has gone to the dogs yet again.
He promised me a lifetime.

And now they're telling me
he can't keep his word?
That decades have rotted into weeks.
That half of me has decayed into grief
that I'll visit once a month on a Sunday with nothing
but fresh flowers and tears to talk over.
And I can't do anything to stop that?

I can't do anything to stop that.
But I can cut his hair.

His wall of hair
that stood so strong when we first met.
Strong enough to withstand me.
And mortgage payments.
It survived the first round of chemo
but the second time it fell down.
Weak from fighting for democracy.
And when they told him that he had lost, you see
his hair began to grow back. And when it did,
it was white.
Just like he'd promised.
All of the things he had promised
- the future
the retirement, the grey –
now sit on top of his head.

And so now I cut his hair.
He tells me how it wants it
and I know people don't think it looks very good
but he tells me that I've done a great job.
And I can have that.

We can make our small bit of future
look how we want it to.
And we can have that.'

TOBY CAMPION

WINTER

White knuckle grips. Pen, pencil, seizure.
She writes with the same intensity: –
Shopping list, billet de jour, shipping note,
Work report, poem, ransom note, resignation,
Marriage lines, death warrant, blank cheque,
Pause to breathe, to remember, to regret, to write.
Rem . . .
Ancient withered oak, leafless, naked.
Spread-eagled, entwined, knotted branches.
Black cloak and claw. Lines and lies and libel.
Warning signs, omens, signals and symbols.
Caw, caw, caw!
Unblinking eyes, hypnotic, haunting, hunted.
Cold stare.
Thaw.
Ice melts only at the end of the page. Inky trail.
Thoughts and emotions, tracks, derailed,
Devoured by a timeless blushing sky.
Re-engaging conversation, meaningless words,
The here and how, and how and how?
That was then,
That was her.

AMELIA MICHAEL

THE FORTUNE TELLER

I have looked into the future through the dim glass of our day
While the past is flowing backwards and the present fades away.
New homes will be discovered, planet children of a star.
But no one there will venture, it is infinitely far.

And the liquid gold will vanish while the users search in vain
For that which now is used and gone cannot return again.
And the smallest will be greatest, they will slay a multitude.
For the smallest are the wisest using everything as food.

And that which lives five hundred years is toppled in a day.
For it which takes a poisonous gas will give the same away.
A land awaits destruction with both grief and tears widespread,
When rippling waves of Mother Earth leave wounded and the dead.

There are vast climatic changes and the sea usurps the land
Apocalyptic horsemen roam the world and will command
Floods spread to new horizons, swollen rivers overflow
Tornadoes ravage landscapes and all nature seems the foe.

When magnetic poles are changing so the south becomes the north,
When Aurora Borealis fails to send its signals forth.
There is then a time of crisis with a penetrating ray,
When the night will be a shelter and the enemy – the day.

A traveller from the realms of space will hurtle through the air
He heralds visitation with huge thunder roll and flare
There will come – maybe tomorrow, mountains tremble, burst and burn
When the Arctic ice for many years will gather and return.

The seeds of our destruction are found within us all,
As the population rises while necessities will fall.
And the future is robotic, figures come and we obey,
For they come without a conscience and we cannot say them nay.

Fortune teller, Nostradamus, gifted with the second sight
Saw some visions of the future – clouded with the depths of night.
Did he see a new tomorrow – as the shadows move away?
For the world a new beginning? Will there be a better day?

There are always Doomsday prophets, do not think there's no avail,
Trust your gods and go on homewards – just a fortune teller's tale.

ROBERT CAIRNS-HARRISON

SNOWFLAKES

She stands with hands facing upward: palms showing. And with cheeks glowing,
her big brown eyes explore each face as if it were a flake of snow.
And she smiles: The way she did the first time she learned
That every single snowflake is unique. Like you. Unique.

And as she looks at you, as she searches every mute mouth
for the words you wish you'd said and the stories you've never told,
know that even though you may not meet again;
even though you may not speak,
and even though she may not ever know your name. She loves you.

But listen:
Atticus said, 'You never really know a man until you have walked a mile in his shoes,'
and she's spent years in other people's shoes:
Roaming other realities, running risks for no reason
other than to chase someone else's rainbow.
Telling someone else's story.
Maybe her own shoes just never seemed to fit.

But listen:
She can tell you why the girl in Class 3I with the big blue eyes
and the cheekbones is scared
when boys flatter and stare, and why she never lets them walk her home.
Listen, and she can tell you why the smile on the woman at the bar
can beam so bright it burns each retina it reaches,
but never lights her own eyes with its warmth.
She can tell you why the man next door,
who sees existence as coincidence and nothing more than that,
although he laughs at Lady Luck when she comes in,
still salutes the lonely magpies in the spring.
She can tell you. Will you listen?

Because Orwell said, 'All are equal,' but I guess it's true
that some are more 'equal' because the ring in her nose
and the stud in her cheek mean that every time she tries to speak,
someone says, 'No. Not her.'
They stare at that hairstyle: Pixie cut, candyfloss pink,

and they turn their back on those big, brown eyes convinced, I think,
that hair dye has coloured her opinions,
and that it shows more about her than her eyes do.
Convinced, I think, that piercing means piercing flesh and logic,
and that it says more about her than her words do.

And maybe that's true.
But to her, you will always be flakes of snow,
with pasts she longs to get to know because that's the closest
she'll ever get to touching the untouchable.
To her, you are utterly beautiful. Completely unique.

So, in a society where 'you' are the size of your stomach
and the shade of your skin
before you are the depth of your compassion.
In a time when 'you' are the holes in your flesh
before you are the gaps in your knowledge,
and the chemicals in your hair before you are the smile in your eyes.
Will you listen to a girl who sees only snowflakes?

SARAH PARKER

RISE AND FALL

The Earth tilts and
summer loosens its fat fingers
one by one, and slowly slides over the edge.
Before it falls it grabs
at the thin arc of blue glass,
pulling down its shrieking, crystal sharpness
as it drops
into the ink.
There is a hush.
Heated ground deflates.
Without its acrylic coating
colours start to leak out of leaves,
draining from landscape like bath water.
Flickering, silvered lances
drip magma, liquid amber,
acid apples, figs and flame.
Glycerin green melts down every supple stem.
Edges start to curl,
folding over and into themselves.
Hollow, twisting, papery creatures,
breath light and brittle,
skin pulled taught between rib and backbone.
They crush to dust,
leaving perfect, skeletal tracings.
All this collects at our feet
as life sucks back into the earth.
Then dampness creeps in.
It cannot be stopped.
It rises up and falls
in lacy waves.
Pinprick moisture
fuses to faces,
fills lungs,
brings sky to ground.
Soft, airbrushed shapes,
seal-grey, smoke wood,
smothering distance,

rotting sound,
narrowing purpose.
It languishes lazily outside,
tapping persistently at the sugar-thin glaze
of our comfortable, electric lives,
yawns a millimetre from our watertight nests,
and waits.
And all the while razor wire roads and paths
constrict around the world.
A tangled string of lights,
scratching a blaze of red and silver trails
as we come and go.

NATALIE WU

NARCISSUS

I'm a poet he said
and he tossed his head
and I must say he looked the part.
With his wistful face and his air of grace
just right for breaking my heart.
He was moody and glum
and he sucked his thumb
in his coat of velveteen
my heart was enraptured, my spirit was captured
and I said things I wanted to mean.
His shirt was cream with a ruffled seam
his hair was curly and fair
my spirit yearned and my psyche burned
with a flame if he wasn't there.
I'm a lover he said so I took him to bed
and I must say he wasn't bad
he could charm the birds with his honeyed words
he could make you laugh or be sad.
He would tell me tales about Celtic Wales
he enthralled me for hours on end.
My heart was aflame when he spoke my name
in the poems and letters he'd send.
Our passion lasted all summer long
but it died at the winter's touch
I could finally see that he couldn't love me
cos he loved himself too much . . .

JAN PRICE

THE OFFICE FRIDGE

The fridge is somewhere cool and calm
You'd think in this office it would come to no harm
But something is lurking in the deep dark realm
Oh help, something is moving deep within its helm
The fridge mafia jump up with glee
Yippee, it's time to do a fridge cull spree
It's Friday, it's time, it's 4 o'clock!
Roll up your sleeves, let work take the knock
Sweaty lettuce, ham that mings
Dripping cucumbers, yoghurt that sings
'Let me out, let me out'
The stinky foodstuffs do shout
I'm well past my sell-by date
I've been stored here since 1988
You've broken the golden, sacred rule
You've been unkind, so heartless, so cruel
The fridge can't do its sterile job with any passion
When you pile up 50 cheeses in a higgledy-piggledy fashion
You are what you eat, the healthy-ites say
In that case, there's no chance
Best throw the manky lot away!

JANE DOWSON

WEEPING WILLOW

Far, far away in the Land of Blue Willow
where bells peal at midnight and wolves howl at dawn
and snow falls in summer on curly-peaked mountains
where cuckoos build nests and black tigers are born.
In silvery shadows of silky grey chiffon
with greeny-blue espadrilles tattered and torn
embroidered with sequins and peacock-eyes rubies
she stands at her window, my lady forlorn.

She hides from the sun behind icicle curtains
and watches pale willow flowers dance in the breeze.
She waits for a footstep that heralds his coming;
the lover returning, whom nobody sees
but the blue shadow lady. She sighs in delusion
of constant devotion whence all reason flees,
and lifts up her face for the kiss of her dreaming;
exquisite delight amid whispering trees.

And down in the depth of the night's eerie darkness
where tightly wound clocks holding time in their hands,
shall release pent-up clangour and waken the witches
to spell out their curses with wavering wands.
Wild wizards and warlocks command apparitions
to weave a fine trousseau and forge golden bands
to fit the slim finger of she who would wed –
in her flawed understanding of shimmering sands
- that lover who left her to live with another
where no willows grow in some far distant lands.

At the foot of the bell-tower she spreads out her mantle
then laughs as the cuckoo eggs fall from the sky;
and hanging her harp at the top of the willow tree
weeps once again for a sign from on high
while music comes trickling from boulder-filled rivers
like sounds of pure happiness running away
'neath frail bamboo bridges with porcelain people
and glaciers splinter to startle the day
into shattered illusions, and pitiless sunshine

bears down without mercy on lovers who cry
at reality's harshness, their hands clasped together.

Yet; cuckoos *will* roam and lovebirds *will* fly.

My Blue Willow Lady grows colder in daydreams
till, climbing her bell-tower and waiting to die,
she offers oblations and prayers to Diana
resigned to her future with sob and a sigh.

BARBARA YOUNG

LAMB TO THE SLAUGHTER

As I tell you the tale of my grandfather's daughter,
My memories of whom have all started to rust,
You must know that my words are like salt in the water.

She used to be bright with all that the world brought her,
Yet now she surveys it with naught but disgust,
As I tell you the tale of my grandfather's daughter.

She fixates on transient things that were taught her,
Insists that all changes be met with mistrust.
You must know that my words are like salt in the water.

It seems like the traps that the years have laid caught her
And she howls at the clocks that her share was unjust,
As I tell you the tale of my grandfather's daughter.

Long since have I waited, so long have I sought her;
Though my love lies encased in a mountain of dust,
You must know that my words are like salt in the water.

Fear of change is what leads her, like lamb to the slaughter,
To the block where an axe cleaves the wood in one thrust.
As I tell you the tale of my grandfather's daughter
You must know that my words are like salt in the water.

DAN HARTIGAN

THAT EMBARRASSING URGE

Oh dear! It's coming back again,
That torment which is not a pain
But which, like pain, must be endured
Until, like pain, it can be cured.
Yet no one in the room must guess
The genesis of my distress.
I tell myself it isn't real –
That this discomfiture I feel
Can be suppressed by power of will . . .
It doesn't work. I feel it still.
It's getting more insistent now.
It must be remedied somehow.
Perhaps some discreet squirming might
Be just enough to ease my plight
Without my being judged to be
Embarrassingly fidgety.
But no. The surreptitious squirm
Is out. My seat is too infirm;
Of all the chairs, this one's unique:
The slightest movement makes it squeak,
And chiding eyes are turned to see
What caused that rude discordance – me!
Oh Lord! I know that I'll go mad
If there's no respite to be had.
The speaker's going on and on,
My interest has long since gone,
Quite overwhelmed by my dismay.
I only want to get away.

At last! *At last!* I'm free to go.
The greatest pleasure that I know
Awaits without: some private place
Where, finally, without disgrace,
I'll ashamedly succumb
And scratch – ecstatically! – my bum.

ALAN BIGNELL

MUM

Which way was I looking when I lost my mother?
What second did she leave?
I never noticed.
Perhaps I did not wish to see the sending money
to countless so-called charities.
Crooks who took her pension and took advantage.
The day she turned left instead of right when she exited the bank,
a place she had visited for over fifty years,
withdrawing and replacing meagre amounts.
When she returned, pale and thirsty on swollen purple feet,
having walked for hours on sun-seared pavements,
she could not explain.
I made her tea, relieved she was home.
We were together but alone.

This year, Mum forgot my birthday.
I wasn't sad the day had slipped her mind,
just upset she could no longer remember the cakes she had baked
on stifling August afternoons,
bent over the cooker, melting chocolate.
The gifts she had saved for but could ill-afford.
Tiny silver ballet shoes on a chain.
A wicker sewing basket and silk threads
with which to reweave broken dreams.
I wonder, are her memories stowed away,
the key broken in the lock?
Or have they slipped away unseen,
like shadows silently escaping underfoot?
I shared my cake, happy she was safe, in my home.
We were together but alone.

'My mum is sharp. Never misses a trick. She's not ill.
She's old,' I reassured.
'I'll get it in a minute,' she cried,
struggling to recall my daughter's name.
'It begins with S,' said Sophie.
'Susie?' Mum replied, recalling the name of her first pet.
Retired from her paper round aged 80,

her job every day for thirty years, hands smeared with newsprint,
walking the streets, delivering to those who never knew her face,
who did not care when she slipped and fell on pavements
laminated with ice, so long as they didn't have to risk their necks.

When she got pneumonia, she refused to eat or drink.
Three doctors came. She turned her head away.
And I cried in the kitchen, arguing with my father on the phone:
'Call you? How can I talk to you when my mum is too sick to speak?'
'Want me to say something to her?'
Ten years estranged and never a word between them.
I often wonder what he said.
But I did hear her reply: 'Okay, darling. Yes, I will.'
The man she had loved all her life had made it right
but they never spoke again.
I made her tea. She drank it.
We were together, both of us, alone.

'Talk to me, Mum.' My words falling like stones into the sea.
I want her back, the woman who made me.
The woman who made me who I am.
Whoever that may be.
I smile, she nods, I make her tea.
She forgets to drink it. We are together.
Soon, I will be alone.

JOAN ELLIS

SHE SLEEPS

I wake up early most morning times
to fret about this and that inside my head,
Accumulating tiredness, while she lies,
serene, a dream playing with her eyelids
and now and then a corner of her mouth.
In moments of doubt, I shake her wrist
or touch her lips and she wakes,
in a riot of eyelashes, flashing
the loss of connection to the
night story, her hair a honey glory
of curls swirling across the pillow,
perfectly placed so her face rises
right in the middle, where she left it last night.

There is a moment, just a moment,
moving from one world to the other,
when she seems unsure of whether
she should push through to the new day,
play a ray of light to help the sun along;
or slip back into the soft folds of the
old night's incantations which have
enchanted and cleansed her. She
usually decides, nearly arrived, to stay,
ready to be provider, adviser, a shoulder,
a foot soldier in each day's denial
of the negative, the grey, the single file.
She is a shepherdess of human hearts.

And when she's weary after each allotted
task is done, and the sand of a day has
long plunged down the narrow gap by which
acts that come from love alone
should be allowed to pass, I
ask myself whether it is right to
burden her when sleep calls. Sometimes
I stare at two dark walls or across
the room to a lowered blind, find
peace of mind in knowing she has

prayed for me, in her own way, and so
join her in her journeys through riddles we've set
in waking hours, by leaving much unsaid.

Which leads to thoughts of bed, the night-time
chessboard, each game played in pairs, where
combinations of pieces, awake and sleeping,
guess and out-guess the others, then themselves.
They dig and delve into a shifting void of
untold, un-dared desires and requirements that
litter the emptiness, unsure as to where to go,
what to try, whether to fall or fly, whom to seek out.
Such are my thoughts, somewhere between the
night's black and white. I think I am there alone,
most of the time; and as the sun begins to buy the day,
I see the peace in the new lines in the new face
and know who won at chess in just one move.

PETER TAYLOR

BENEFIT CLAIMANT

A full-time mum, in full-time work,
training to be a nurse,
I am a benefit claimant.

Running home from the train in the rain
carrying bags in freezing hands
from the discount stands
of the supermarket aisles –
hoping to raise a smile at home
with dirt cheap horse meat sausage rolls,
wishing I had the choice
to buy something that would really
fill the holes.

The paper-thin walls of my chipboard house
can't keep out the accusatory shouts
that I am a leech on this country's wealth
and I have done this to myself.
I am a benefit claimant.

You tell me that I waste my benefit cheques
on drink and smokes and big TVs –
you think those are my luxuries.
But a luxury to me is turning on the heating
when you can see your breath in the kitchen;
a luxury is eating meat twice a week
and knowing that your roof won't leak;
and being able to pay for the prescription
that you need to feel human.

A luxury is feeling human
when you see your lifestyle maligned
in the headlines
and you are called a waste of time
on prime-time TV.
I am a benefit claimant.

If you want me to pay back
your hard-earned tax
that I don't deserve,

you are welcome
to my unbranded cereal flakes,
my blunt razor blades
and my single glazed windowpanes,
my trainers with holes in the soles:
you can take it all.

Or maybe you could give me
the benefit of the doubt
that I need the benefits for now
but I am working my way out.
I am a benefit claimant.

ROSIE STEWART

THEY'RE MURDERERS, NOT MUSLIMS

Amid the chaos of screams and sirens
confusion reigns.
City of love becomes a hellhole of hatred
and the world will never be the same –
indeed many won't ever be seen again,
lives wasted in an orgy of spite
designed to stir a backlash, make us fight
against decent people of belief,
to justify more sickening deeds
when extremists can claim they're right,
recruiting more brainwashed fools
to drown in pointless pools of blood.

So many fall into the trap,
turn on Muslims who despise this crap,
insanity that spreads across the map
as they see their faith being hijacked
by the mentally unstable.
Such nightmares cannot be curbed
until we note the absurdity
of following the thoughtless herd,
engage our brains, let decency be heard.

I am an atheist and proud,
will shout out loud that I'm an infidel.
But Muslims, I respect you.
Christians, Hindus, Jews
and all others too.
As individual human beings
I love you till you give me reason not to.

Bigots, racists, xenophobes.
You feed the beast.
Remove the blinkers, take a look at facts
and see the real brutes for what they are
not what propaganda tells you.

Remember what the Daily Mail said
about European Jews in thirty-nine.
They're playing the same card now in a different suit.
Refugees didn't commit the horror in France
though some will take the chance to bend the truth
and tell you something else.
If ever Britain faces catastrophe
and you feel the need to flee
you'll no doubt see it as your right
to take flight anywhere you choose.
Just hope they let you through
not take a quick suspicious look at you
and say you're not a refugee
but an opportunist killer
continuing Blair's legacy.

CLIVE OSEMAN

CHAI

I think
some people
like people
just like
milk

pure
white
and homogenised

But I want chai

I want to marvel at
cloves, cinnamon and cardamom
singing in perfect harmony

I want to bear witness
to the marriage of
normal-i-tea and spices

Let the delightful flavours of diversity
dance playfully on my tongue
before watching them honeymoon
through the milk of human kindness
with sugar always at hand to keep things sweet

I don't want proper tea
politely sitting in tiny cups
patiently waiting
to be sullenly sipped
from pursed lips

I want
fiery chai
ferociously bubbling
over the pot
because it has yet
to be forced
to believe in
boundaries.

CHRISTINA O'SULLIVAN

WALK WITH FLASHLIGHT

Through double gates, a track of slimy stones
slide to the reservoir:
source of the chill,
cause of comfortless
fan heaters on full. Neither wine nor pill
will settle restless spirits.

I had thought the gleam of animal eyes
scorched by torchlight would provide
what's needed: Soul food.
Nothing emerges but owl-less, scuttle-less dark.
Darkness set like concrete, meat-thick.
A slab, a parody of moorland

painted by an artist skimming the surface,
accepting surface as internal world:
A day dictated
by clock, hike, flask and pre-packed snack.
The world below your surface
is ungoverned. Turn back.

KITTY DONNELLY

EITHER/OR

Creme Eggs provide unhealthy distaste for revenge
A revenge of betrayal, fate and isolation
Sit listening to the skipping record crackling smoke
Quiet corner draws the curtains to quarter silence
Striped underwear sheds light on night queen's disposition
Reject outward self in pursuit of inner peace
Calm before the storm shifts similes as moonbeams
Pick apart your friends with real skill
To know means to destroy all relations to infinity
Flippant climax revokes trivial pubescent dreams
That canvas my love bright as marigold gloves
In a basket of light listened to understandably explicit
Murmuring words because there's nothing left to say
We belong together like a cliché saccharine song
Stalking originality as a virgin dressed in black
Clinching love whilst mending broken seams
I readdress a chemical imbalance staring into a dream.

LIBA RAVINDRAN

HALF-FULL

I am listening.
But the constant pounding of melancholy is
like salty waves crashing against a sea wall
subtly eroding the defences.
As I absorb the negativity
I crumple, concertina;
crushed, like a toothless gurning shadow of who I really am.
Insides tainted blue, like the swirling ink of a leaking pen.
How can I convince you the chalice is half-full
when my own vial is slowly seeping?

SIGRID MARCEAU

CONNECT THE DOTS

I write on scraps
And weathered pages.
I jot down raps
And picture stages.
I write down dreams
And go through phases.
I wish to be,
A chain of daisies.

Love me.
Forget me not.
Cover me in lots of
Drops of
Tangled
Sticky knots of
Nature's nectar.

Sweet sap drips.
Ink's an ancient script.
This letter to my heart
Sparks a one-way trip,
Down a slow winding path;
Through a beautiful park,
Where the day
Meets the dark
In the dawn
Of my mind.

In the maze of my brain,
I can travel through time,
I can move in straight lines
From today
To tomorrow.
Through the rain
On the planes,
And the rainbows
That follow.

I can jaunt
Back to the future.
To the depths
Of the hollows.
Where the Song
Of the Swallows,
Is played by Apollo.

I can replay
Every living memory.
From this life,
Past lives,
And even
Future histories.
I'm travelling
Through centuries.

My cells are
Filled with memories
And fuelled by
Past life energies.
My ancestry,
Genetically,
Connected.

See, I'm predisposed
To memories
And energies,
My conscious mind
Has never seen.
Has never felt.
Has never known.

Subconsciously,
I know these scenes.
I see them
In my restless dreams.
In deep REM sleep,
Connected to
These memories;
I remain
In this wonderful maze.

Rewind,
Pause,
Play,
Fast forward.

Memories are everlasting.
Ever after.
Even after
Lifetimes pass;
And the atoms of
The souls' shell part;
They move and fuse
To form new life.
In new forms.
With new norms.

But the day,
Is the same day.
And the dawn,
Is the same dawn.
And the sun sets,
In the same place.
And the storms form,
In the same way.
And the Earth rests,
In the same space.

I am but a speck.

A dot.

What is the meaning?
Or at least what say I?

Look for love.
Look for light.
Look for nothing outside.
Look within,
Third eye,
And you'll connect
The dots.

Oneness will embrace you
As you perch upon
The moon,
Taking in the view
Of this great spectacle
We like to call,
Life.

ESI YANKEY

WE ARE THE SKY

Dark clouds hang ominously o'erhead
Shrouding clear vantage of mind an' heart
Casting rose-tinted life into utter blackness
With no foreseeable escape from dark

Stood sentinel, with laboured duty
I have watched your gradual slip away
Into the thunderous clouds that overshadow
Long sleepless nights and callous bitter days

Though blessed life becomes you
Cruel depression grasps too strong
Clings a limpet 'pon a beaten rock
Bides an unwelcome guest, whom doth prolong

With regret I offer no armoured dress
To flank delicate skin, and so protect
And I gift no gallant weaponry
To defend this civil unrest

But I offer you my love
I extend to you strong arms
And I pledge that they shall hold you close
Until electric storms do calm

I will drape you in mine own skin
Made thick enough for two
And I beg please seek the light in me
For it can guide you through

I shall speak to you with only truth
Obscuring clouds cannot belie
For these clouds, are naught but passing clouds
But together, we are the sky.

HELEN MATHER ROGERS

EVERY BEAT

With every beat there is the need
For the fluid of life to flow
Beating with erratic motion
Then, when this fault occurs
The fear of death steps in.
When the fear of failure strikes
Burning thoughts confuse the mind
What will life's future bring?
What burden will they be to bear?
When stress and will anxiety pounds.
Reality strikes like a burning flame
We are left with many questions
Why have things suddenly gone astray?
Were we careful and exercised the necessary care?
Did we take the ultimate precaution
To protect the value of life's every beat?
Did we treat what we were granted
Like a treasured possession, a precious gem?
Did we forget it was only on loan
Without a deposit and no payments to repay?
It had to be returned when its earthly work was done
Why did we abuse it and overuse it?
And it failed to serve us well
What now? When failure strikes?
And the fluid ceases to flow
The engine splutters and dies
When there's no recourse and no repair
When the valve of life beats no more.

BURGESS JAY BARROW

THESE STREETS

I was born here, under Maggie's rule;
living beneath her Spitting Image character,
hanging from a telecom wire overhead.
The youth here knew hate before they knew love
and everybody hated the Iron Lady.
Everything here was grey; from the rows of well-worn
tenements and dirt-strewn streets
to the sunken eyes of every battered wife.
Violence was rife, accepted as normality,
a messed-up reality that you were more of a man
if you used your fists or feet on a regular basis.
Even if it was taking a liberty by terrorising
the mother of your children. Beating your own wife
for fun or frustration, usually after a Friday night in the boozer,
tanked up on cheap beer. Or maybe after a day at the bookies
where you spanked the message money on a dead-cert at Doncaster.
It was always the wife that got the blame.

Then there were the football casuals;
young boys who thrived on the blood of their rivals.
Organised chaos for teenage kicks.
Most of them were too buzzed on cheap glue
to feel the shards of broken glass
being picked out of their punk-styled hair
by the bloodied hands of their weeping mothers.
Too messed up on drugs and booze to consider
the poor woman who had to leave her other kids at Christmas
to visit her thug of a son in HMP Barlinnie.

This was 1980s Glasgow. This is where I was born,
and it was a life that most could never comprehend.
These streets were made for nothing,
and for as long as I can remember, I knew,
that I was never made for these streets.

HELEN ELLIOTT

TRANSFORMATION

He'd found the eggs on a clump of nettles
At four pm on the nineteenth of May.
(All very neatly chronicled of course,
Being meticulous about such things)
Ignoring the pain of the plant's revenge,
He moved the clump to the tank in his room
And, completely deaf to the outside world,
He watched, day after day, 'Jack, it's dinner.'
'Won't be long, I think one's started changing.'
He missed the first one on the eighth of June;
It happened sometime during double maths.
But, on the ninth of June, he watched in awe
As number two emerged and then two more.
'Mum, look at this; they've reached the larva stage.'
'That's lovely dear. Come on, it's shepherd's pie.'
For weeks they chomped on the plants provided,
Black bodies, speckled white, they swelled each day,
While he chronicled their evolution.
Until, with mouth agape, he noted them
Weaving their bodies into silk cocoons.
'They're pupas now Mum, one more stage to go.'
For two long weeks he waited eagerly,
While one of nature's miracles occurred.
And then, with chin in hands, he stared, bewitched,
As one, and then another, struggled free.
A few hours as they gathered up their strength
Before the first one made its maiden flight.
He saw it flapping at the windowpane.
'They're flying; I told you they were peacocks.'
Then, very gently, with his chronicle,
He nudged it upwards to the open air.
Joyfully it fluttered through, circled once
And made a beeline for the buddleia.

BRYN STRUDWICK

THIS IS YOUR TWENTIES

This is your twenties:
Thank God for Facebook, emails and mobile phones
Because if we were landlines and Filofaxes
Everything would be scribbled out three times –
'Till we switched to pencil for everyone.
Each page crumpling under the weight of its history:
Each erased address a ghost of a house share.
Forwarding addresses and forgotten postcodes.

This is your twenties:
Postcodes make good additions to passwords.
A technie taught you that
Seven jobs ago.

This is your twenties:
The impermanence isn't painful *per se*:
But it takes something from you;
This lack of solid ground.

This is your twenties:
And you are one of the urban nomads
Lives organised by smartphones
And scuppered by batteries or broken screens.

This is your twenties:
And 'Goodness, you've got a . . . diverse CV.
Can you talk it through with me?'
Listen, hundredth recruiter, if it looks scrappy
It's because there are just scraps of jobs going.

This is your twenties:
How did you lose so many nights?
How did you gain so many biros?
A detritus gathering that you need to get clean of
- And you will –
Just as soon as you find the time.

This is your twenties:
You're in the prime of your life
But you've now had more jobs than sexual partners
And you think you might be doing this wrong.

This is your twenties:
Music and memories are digitised or discarded
Because who has room for hard copies?

This is your twenties:
And you're sure that dead laptop
Had something important on it
But it's moving time again:
So keep or throw?

This is your twenties:
Your years of experience are growing into something harder:
Not quite armour,
But people seem to think you're equipped now.

This is your twenties:
Crises typed for broadcast in the small hours
Agonies answered with animal GIFs
Because our loved ones are always reachable
But usually too far away
To give us a hug.

This is your twenties:
Every object aching with memories
And each one a burden as you box and unbox –
Moving from postcode to postcode
And pick where to plant your roots
This season.

This is your twenties:
And every next step could be The One
Where you find the job with the pension scheme you'll actually use,
Or the person you'll grow old with
But each maybe is scattered across your CV:
Each pension contribution cooking in pots too small to keep track of,
Each nearly-there relationship reminding you how close
- And yet how far –
You are
From ever finding

Home.

HANNAH CHUTZPAH

A GLIMPSE

She wanted to experience death
And then return to life;
She thought that this would give her
A glimpse of the other side.
She even bought a casket
And put it in a room;
One night she climbed into it,
The darkness like a tomb.
The lid came slowly down,
Her skin was rather pale;
Then she felt the permanence:
The hammer and the nail.
'This wasn't what I wanted,'
She regretfully did say,
'My visit was for just a glimpse;
I didn't want to stay!'

JEAN AKED

WINGS

Fading light, the evening's wild designs
And twilight cuts the purple sky in lines
The stars are just beyond our fingertips
Dry and cracked the sorry smile upon your lips
Time and life and other wasted things
My sister said,
'I wonder where you hide your wings?'
And another angel sings:
So pointless now the blaming game
'Cause truth and lies hurt just the same
Makes me catch my breath and cry
Takes me back to moments shared in times gone by
When all around the tears are falling
And the world of dreams is calling
As pressure builds, the tourniquet is tightening,
At tunnel's end, the light is brightening
Right here, right now, the dark is deep and frightening
Even so, you cannot take the blame
I loved you then and love you now the same.

MICHELE AMOS

THEFT OF TIME – RUSH-HOUR, CHARING CROSS STATION, THE STAND W.C.1

(My Dad, Our Differences And His Dementia)

'Do I know you?' I touch your arm.
You are sitting.
Straight-backed,
bottle in hand,
rocking.
Hard station concourse.
Ass frozen.
A puddle of piss.
Shocking.

Commuters running. The 18.06 to Crouch End.
Mutter,
invisible,
ringtones utter,
zombies with iPads,
immune.
Laughter mocks your mind.
Spittle from your mouth like it escaped
too soon.

A young girl at your side dabs your chin.
Her voiceless cries
hiding blowjob lies,
wiping her dreams away
in a tissue.
Mother's locket.
Love in another way.

Her eyes, too old, search yours,
find mine
for a film replayed.
Bites the lip
of a childhood washed away.

A patchwork quilt,
one bed,
two lives.
One new day
. . . anyway.

'This man is you.'
The young girl sighs
holding up my head.
I see the stranger in her eyes.
Reflected tears.
A past.
Goodbyes.

I sit down at her side. Your whore?
My child?
Find this man I do not know
whose loves I can't relive,
the dead,
and thoughts which never die.
Strange friends.
And sleep.
A tangle.
Living in my head

We laugh a lot, raise a bottle,
toast our lives.
Dance.
Nursery rhymes.
Cheap red wine.
The best of times,
though . . .
as dawn breaks my new friends go
leaving scary people
who I don't know.

I see the pearly gates ajar.
Funny photos,
tired frames.
Illusions grey,
Lavender.

Instead,
the smell of too much time
tugging us along to meet their mates . . .
Me and you,
and merry-go-rounds.
So much love unsaid.

TORGE UGUR

THE LONDON UNDERGROUND

With frantic speed the human race,
Push and shove to get a space.
Through the open doors they rush
Staggering in the heavy crush.
From the darkened platform roars
A hollow voice of 'Mind the doors'!
A sudden jolt and we're packed in tight,
Breathing in with all our might.
We thunder through the blackened tube,
In air and heat so thick and crude.
'We're here!' I gasp with great relief,
A station full of more good grief!
'There's no more room,' a man implies,
'You're on my toes,' another cries.
I'm almost forced on someone's lap,
A mystery voice yells, 'Mind the gap!'
There really must be another way,
To reach my office every day.
As long as I am still alive,
Maybe tomorrow I'm gonna drive.

PATRICIA GUEST

THE DANCING DECOY

There's a line inside my mind
that my thoughts dance with sometimes,
I never know where it is
or how to avoid it
but when it happens, I can't fail to notice.

Heart is a hammer
rattling the cage,
mind moving faster
fumbling through each page,
never quite discovering
what I'm searching for,
just knowing that when I find it
dust will settle, cool the core.

There's a line inside my mind
that becomes a swing-rope sometimes,
the inner me
will never flee
just feel the burn, whilst gripping tightly.

Train careering off its track
slips and races down my back,
shivers chasing up my spine,
can't place the source of it this time . . .

There's a line inside my mind
crossing another, forming a bind,
I might never get it
or make sense of it,
what causes it
or forces it
to close a bit
and tighten in,
constricted and frightening,
but when it's happening
the only thing
that can be done
to force a draw,

or force a door,
is plan a distraction;
the escape clause.

And so I dive into the moment
earphones in, feeling hopeless,
'til the notes are all I'm breathing
open-mouthed, because I'm singing,
just can't help it anymore
not about to lose the war,
choreograph moves to the kettle
motown, funk or heavy metal?
No one cares, and nor do I,
when I'm dancing in the sky.

I'm lost, it's working,
hands still burning,
but mind barely churning –
now I've chosen to deploy
the dancing decoy!

There's a line inside my mind
that my thoughts dance with sometimes,
it attacks as I unwind,
but if it's a dance it wants
then it's a dance it gets . . .
oh it's not seen my best moves yet!

FRANKIE WILKINSON

DESTROYED

How does it feel to have a noose around your neck?
Thoughts messed up, an emotional wreck.
Hiding in the shadows waiting to die
No one around to see you cry.

A cocktail of pills washed down with drink
No more time to hurt or overthink
Your body begins to slow as your heart skips a beat
Cold and clammy, white as a sheet.

The noose is tight, you jump off the chair
You mutter the words 'life's unfair'
A broken soul, destroyed by words
Finally free to fly with the birds

Slowly you start to slip away.
Couldn't bare to live another day
The pain was all too much for you to cope
Broken-hearted and given up hope.

The darkness lingers long after you're gone
Oh how I wished you could have moved on
You deserved to have a smile on upon your face
Another life that we cannot replace.

LAURA AIMEE

LONGING, ACHING, BURNING

Longing;
For the memory to recede like the tide except,
To not return for I am better left
To my devices and my vices
At night when day seems twice as
Dark and I feel foolish for bearing my stark
Naked soul in the light of a fleeting spark,
The life of which was short-lived
But seemed to span a hundred years.

Aching,
Battered, bruised and grieving something that was once constant
Like the sunrise, sunset and as wanton
As the stars are when they decide
Closed eyes are the place to hide
Midway between consciousness and well-earned dreams,
Is the rain actually as cold as it seems,
Or is this the temperature
Of mourning? Minus one, zero.

Burning
Desire for the truth withheld like flames behind fireproof glass
Fighting, dwindling, surrendering at last
To carbon dioxide lies
That tainted tears from green eyes
Like chemicals spoil rivers, the way vodka
Erodes livers leaving death-woven lokta
Paper, an application
To move on to something better.

Longing. Aching. Burning. Moving
On.

JODIE WALTERS

MY EYES ARE COLOURLESS

My eyes are colourless,
a point-blank gaze
at the human maze,
forever peeled,
going nowhere
in posh leather, heeled high.
Static lids never blink,
today I'm wearing . . . Summer pink,
wish I could wiggle and wink
at that exquisite vision in mink.
Cannot move a muscle
in the high street hustle,
watch every move
of those who groove,
the gin-filled fools,
the beery leery,
the proud, out of closet gay and camp,
a desperate, bereft, seven-layered tramp.
Two AM ten men, in my doorway, leak,
then take the piss of the willowy geeks . . .
Sad sallow-paled youths,
draped in the dark garb of the Goths,
gathered under stark neoned take-out
like a Mac-flurry of moths.
Tongue-tied new courters snog-hog the view . . .
his ex stumbles past . . . crying,
boohoo, boohoo.
Dull dawn brings 'Morning Stan'
council cleaner Supervac man.
Early years mums take tots to playschool
chilled job hunter, Jim, zips up his cagoule,
tight benefit cutbacks, the PM's a tool.
Feisty, shopping-trollied pensioner, Polly
hums to iPod maestro Barbirolli,
struggles to erect her battered brolly.
So here I stand permanently rooted,
changed into an Italian two-piece . . . suited

by the newbie girl with ice-maiden hands,
got to advertise chic current brands.
In the curious rectangle of my sight
displaying the wares
all day and all night . . .
Everything's changeless, nobody cares.
Everything alters, who wins, who dares.
All I can give them?
Emotionless stares.

STEVE DOUGLAS

OH, FOR GOD'S SAKE

How can you treat a square with divinity,
Yet cast your brother as a slave?
The cube has not the aspect
Of a child of God.
The four faces
Of your idol-headed
Tetrahedron,
Could not display
Such random duplicity
At nations do today.
No twelve pentagons
Can create a jury of peers,
No divinity lies in these
Playthings of God.
His marbles
His jangling toys.
Yet in their perfection
Lies the blandness
You seek.
Equal sides?
What does that mean to you?
A Dron shares no equality with a drone,
You lie comfortable with the same,
All the same.
Bland! Blind! Ignorant besides,
You clone people like Platonic shapes
And in abusing terms
Abuse your god,
Unique gems, each little child,
Difference is their perfection,
Beyond your comprehension,
In their difference lies your fear of scope,
You cannot understand
And so you lie.

Each human must be of
Equal shape and size,
Each perfect replication
A dedication to your
Oblivion.

PATRICIA ANN STONE

THE UNTETHERED BALLOON

I had a chance to see how the world was made
high up where nobody crowds the mist
and ground is down at least 1,000 feet;
in the basket of a huge balloon –
if you like, a sort of womb,
a whimsical toy of gods carrying us aloft.

We soared above electric wires
and below, we made the chickens run.
Nailed up only by invisible hot air,
hot air, can you imagine!
People are often full of it
but they never reach such heights.

There must be practical uses for hot air
but I was thrilled to personally discover
that dangling like a flea beneath a balloon
is akin to trembling on God's eyelash,
cruising for a sneak preview of Earth's axis
while brushing treetops –
like being gauze passed around by wind,
and silently outwitting gravity
while a curious cow gazes upward from below,
a questioning 'moo' escaping through her mouth.

Then there was a boy dashing a dark streak
diagonally through a drenched green field;
his thrilled head craned heavenward,
chasing our drift with dew-lashed legs,
a child with fantasy brimming in his lungs.

My life shall not pass without another flight.
Next time, in my floating wonder,
I will bring home a ribbon of cloud
wrapped in a handkerchief of sky –
fully understand why some animals must fly,
and Heaven's always there to give advice.

KAREN EBERHARDT-SHELTON

CEFFYL DWR (WATER HORSE)

It is not easy to enter
The land of beginnings,
Where winds cast spiteful spells
On friendless sea and shore,
Where shadows swallow latter day
And trees entwine in sinister display.
If so, where lies that land?
For wild with illusion my head
Impacts the opacity of silence
Wherein voices, reduced to whispers,
Are borne by blustery storms and dissolve
In waves foaming with riddles.

But there was a land for life, a land for loss,
For Ceffyl Dwr with fiery breath,
Yes for Ceffyl Dwr the water horse
Who, now with seal-like skin, as cold as death,
No longer strides with stretching bay,
A bewildering beast with hooves a-splay.
Yes there was a land where Ceffyl Dwr,
The prankster horse, tricked the lonely traveller
To climb and rest upon its easy frame,
To carry him wild o'er hill and heath
'Til the wingless beast, melting in nightly mists,
Let slip the hapless victim to his death beneath.

GERALDUS JOHN

THE EYE OF PARANOIA

Paranoia, paranoia, paranoia!

Watchful eyes seethe and stare,
Glisten-grey, growl, glare,
Evil eyes spin all around,
Can you hear my heartbeat pumping with sound?

Paranoia, paranoia, paranoia!

Heartbeats bleed a scarlet scream,
The vision of the world appears not as it seems . . .
Eyes surveillance side to side,
No air to run! No air to hide!

Paranoia, paranoia, paranoia!

I reach out for my deep dark soul,
Black as death; dark as coal,
'Save me soul! I'm in despair!
Fiery eyes flame everywhere!'

Paranoia, paranoia, paranoia!

Ferocious fear thoughts collapse,
Symptoms echo deep relapse,
'Ugly!' ruminate voices sneer,
My soul suffocates with panic and fear.

Paranoia, paranoia, paranoia!

Destructive soul, will I survive?
Breathless, burnt, am I alive?
Will you help my soul relive, revive?
Can you resuscitate me back to life?

Paranoia, paranoia, paranoia!

I question the mirror with hatred and fire,
'Mirror, am I beautiful?' screams pain and desire,
'Worthless!'
The eye of paranoia cries,

And as they say the mirror never lies . . .

Paranoia, paranoia, paranoia!
Paranoia, paranoia, paranoia!

NABILAH AFZAL

METEORIC MOMENT

Waking the darkest spheres: a division
Of silence: an explosion
Of bright white flowers
Jumping like astonished eyes in showers
Of dancing diamonds, threading, curling,
Spreading sparks of night lights in whirling
Colours casting chaotic contours
Of patterns, painting scores
Of leaping forms and images:
Of Heavenly passages
That dissolve into a bereavement
In a cloudless black covenant.

ALISON HODGE

BROLLY RAGE

I don't have a reliable umbrella
He always lets me down.
When it's time to do his job
He messes me around.
I feel he's being unfaithful
With his lies he's cheating me.
He says he can protect me from the storm
He can't! It's plain to see.
Just when I think he's behaving
Believe me, I have my doubts.
He clearly does a number on me
He changes, inside out.
It's OK, I know there are others
I'm clearly not alone
Clinging on all hopeless
But, just wait until he gets home.

JOANNA CHAMBERLAIN

NORTHERN TEARS

There, amongst the northern skies,
Tears driven by ghostly squalls
Fall on the blackened, bleak rooftops
Of this northern town, forgotten.
Left to a grey Victorian rot
Decaying factory ceilings collapsing on,
Litter-strewn floors, newspapers decompose
With triumphs from yesteryear
Industrial dust-stained brickwork
Grimy reminder, of the grim past
Haunted dim gaslight probing the fog
Day, night only separated by murky light
A ghostly silence, hangs like a deathly fog
Cloaking lost sounds of dull beating on metal,
Boots tramping over cobbled stones,
The sounds of clocking on, clocking off, no more.

NICK STRONG

THE RAINBOW

I had a dream yesterday.
I glided along sweet rays of sunshine
as the breeze brushed
mellifluous strokes of happiness
into my ears.
I landed at the end of a rainbow.
There in gold bold letters
read the following statement:
'My colours do not determine my character.
All I want is to send parachutes of joy
to shelter those under the rain.'
I saw value in those pensive words.
My colours do not determine my character
and I empathise with the desire
to launch jovial droplets of happiness
into the face of testing times.
I wondered if I too could use words
to signify the way for those yet to discover
that sunshine swims in every rain cloud.
I wondered if I could walk along a path
towards a positive clime,
whilst dropping breadcrumbs to guide some
out of the ghettos of their minds.
I wondered if others could
replicate my actions:
helping closed eyes to see
sunshine in the rain.
Showing that although clouds weep,
sublime sunshine still smiles.
We can all be happy.
We can all dance on the graves of our troubles
like tall grass dances on windswept lands.
We can all smile,
as the rainbow sends us parachutes of joy
to shelter us from the rain.

CARLTON ROSE

EVERY STRIKE TO SYRIA HITS ME IN THE HEART

I hear the planes go over again
As I sit in the same comfy chair
A warm home
Far from the war zone
It's easy to disassociate
When the bloodshed's not here.

But that boom
That thundering reminder,
Every time it goes over
It grows louder
And I can't help but wonder
How many lives it will take,
How I am partly responsible
Though not directly to blame
And I want to stop it
But I don't know how,
I want to make them listen
And put their weapons down.
We live in a dictatorship
Thinly disguised as democracy,
They ask us what we want
Then they do what they want anyway.

We live in a world
Where we are evolved enough
To live together harmoniously
Yet we choose to fight each other endlessly,
What can we do?
How can we bring peace?
The only answer I can see
Is to love each other
Unconditionally
Regardless of difference
In skin or opinion
Hate is like an unloved child

Who doesn't understand affection,
But smother him with enough
And he will break down, accepting.

Compassion is growing,
The seeds have been planted
They just need nurturing
To succeed in what we've started.

GEMMA BAKER

A GOOD DAY IN MY TWENTIES

I only snoozed my alarm twice,
I was actually early for work,
and I remembered to bring my lunch.
I haven't gone overdrawn this week
and I haven't bought any useless shit
that will live under my bed until
my annual clear out.

But my mother is proud of me.

You might have a different definition of
a good day:
you bought a house, you got a pay rise,
and you paid off your credit card
in one payment.

But my mother is proud of me.

She may not brag about me at the golf course,
mostly because she doesn't go
to the golf course.
But my mother is proud of me.
My father smiles when his co-workers
ask after me,
and I believe my sister when she tells me
she understands me.

I know my thirty-year-old self
will have a different definition of
a good day:
the baby slept through the night,
the five-year-old got dressed by himself,
and her husband has just got a promotion.
They are holidaying in Hawaii this year.

I am excited for those good days
the same way
my thirty-year-old self will reminisce about
these good days.

RACHEL GLASS

THE CLONES OF TITHONUS

The clones of Tithonus are cluttering these wards.
A geriatric horror of cicadas chirping.
They are rubbing their brittle bones together, sawing
the air that barrels out the coughs of COPD.

And you! Crows are sitting on your chest. You are
as thin as a sigh, and the air is falling through your fingers
like those specks you see, when sunlight hits the dust.
An invisible pianist, your long fingers are quivering

across anachronistic keys. Dead ivory. Which brings us
on to bones. For I can see your mysteries. The humerus,
the femur, why I could put my fingers round them, for
your flesh is just discoloured lace, hanging on a bag of bones.

Your lovely eyes were grey and sombre; a cloud of thought.
They are emptied out. Occluded. Sinking in your head,
its bony profile thrusting forward, the beaky nose,
the ears that seem to grow bigger by the month. Though in truth

it's you who shrinks. Your flesh is corrugation. It bears the stains
of cellulitis, eczema, in flowing deltas, golden and brown.
I see more of you than I care to. Than you care that I should.
Break break break . . . You are a game. Knucklebones.

And you are a black knuckle, skittling the xylophone of bones.
Life is smashing you to pieces and, like one of Larkin's old fools,
you do not see what stands over you. That's me. Pilate.
Washing his hands. And I am handing them the DNR.

* Tithonus: Aurora asked Zeus to make Tithonus immortal
but forgot to ask for eternal youth;
some say he ended his days as a grasshopper hidden behind golden
doors.

SHIRLEY BELL

GIRLS OF SERENDIPITY

This one is for
The girls who always apologise
The girls who are scared
And feel trapped,
Dream big dreams and cry cold tears.
The girls who have been labelled:
Weird, ugly, pretty, maybe unusual
For the girls who can't fit in, won't fit in
Popular and unpopular
The ones the world thinks they see
But no one really knows
The girls who can't find beauty when
They look in the mirror.
Who are angry at themselves
Mother, Father, the Lord or anyone else
The girls who feel like
They're too worldly to ever be holy
Too strict to ever know freedom
The girls who are trying to find their way
Looking for answers to questions unasked
Looking for love in a place born into sin
And shaped in iniquity. The girls who
Grew up on lust, had hate for breakfast,
Received bouquets of bitterness, slept
In beds of jealousy, covered in blankets
Of lies to protect them from storms of insecurity
On blissful nights filled with drunkenness and pain.
And falling asleep on a stomach full of
Vanity and idolatry. The girls who grew up
And trapped their hurt, pain, confusion, rebellion
In the body of a woman.

This one is for you.
To let you know there is one who saves
One who changes
One who knows
One who understands

And you won't have to undress for him to
See what you have to offer
Before he accepts your offer.
He noticed it in your voice,
Saw it in your stance,
Heard the cry in your heart.
And he understood
He hurt with you

This one is for me.
The broken girl with insecurities
Who never knew she could be of such worth
Found value from the love of the most perfect
And his love healed my wounds.

TUMI MARY

WHAT IF THEY KNEW

Nervous at the school gates
Split fates and faces different
They ate rice with a fork
I with a spoon

My mother spoke her sweet Punjabi
Her sweet, sweet Punjabi
Bended to every dialect
I stood by
Itching to leave

What if they hear her
They'll remember I'm different
They'll ignore my face won't they
They'll ignore her embroidery
They'll ignore her kameez
They'll ignore her shalwar
They'll ignore my name
While they say it so differently

Mama and Abu
Clasping what they can
Of what they left behind
Those melodies and native tongue
On sunrise radio before school
I was itching to turn it down
Close the door quickly
And turn my back on home.

What if they heard where they come from
They'll ignore my ignorance
On pop culture references

They'll ignore my grandmother's broken English
Sounding sweeter than a thousand sonnets in the Queen's
If only I knew how sweet it was
I'd hold her hand a little tighter as she walked me home
Where I'll always have to go

My grandfather scolds me in Urdu

It burns twice
One for the scold
One for the Urdu, one for the shame
I'm hoping he stops
They can't ignore that voice

What if they hear his journey
What if they hear the noble decision
What if they hear prison
What if they hear Paris in the winter
What if they hear England spitting him out
What if they hear him swimming
What if they hear Europe
What if they hear England saying come back
What if they hear him running

What if they hear the reason I'm here.

JAMAL MEHMOOD

A WEE SWALLAY

Aim pust, aim pust, a hae a thust – ye's mebby gusd?
Me brekfust heera's a wee Buckfust
A ken um pust – burell tullya thus
N'ull dae ma bust, tay tullya just
Tha wee it wuss – wi that wee lus – apon tha bus.

Aim on the bus! Aim on the bus! – Ach! It's nothin' but heep err rust!
A see yon lassy's heavin' bust
A heavin' bust she laks tay thrust.
Un ye cun trust am no the fust, ta hae a lust fair thut wee bust.
Und she's nay fussed. Aim sturrin' doon lak ull the rust. A hae a lust!

Aye she's nay fussed! She's nay fussed tay faind um pust –
Am no the wust, am no the wust!
She smails – an noo I feel um blust!
She's brusht herr hund agin ma rust.
Teh chairums nay lust! The chairums nay lust!

She's lain heer heed agin ma chust
Ma hairt is poondin' fit tay bust
Und she's weel pust und um weel pust
Und weel . . . it's lak a keenda trust – thuts just – between the tay ovus.
Und then . . .
We kusd!

Och! But noo the morment's lust!
There's nay mair trust, there's nay mair trust
An ull becuss I hay a lust – get oota here wee succubus!
A hay a lust, und so . . . I uskt . . . ye's mebby gusd?
An noo she's gud – she kens am just lak ull tha rust – there's nay mair trust.
Um no the fust, um no the lust!
Um just –

Another jorb.
A feel herr hund aroond me knorb!
She geeza a rob! She geeza a rob
Tha name a Gord! Tha name a Gord!
She's putt ma knorb inseed err gorb!
A gee tha lussie . . . therty borb.

Aim no the fust, aim no the lust
Ach! Thus wees that's wuss tay earn a crust!
Und she's nay fussed, aye she's nay fussed,

But wut is thus?
Um cust! Um cust!
Und just as aim aboot tay bust . . .
Uv nay mair lust! Uv nay mair lust!

And no! It's no becuss um pust. It's just . . . a cannae!
A have nay lust.
Und no! It's no tha thirty borb –
A cannae just . . . a cannae just . . .
Uv nay mair lust!
Ull tullya thus! The noo . . . ma lust . . . is just . . . disgust –
Becuss . . .
We kusd!

Um oot the bus, um oot the bus! A told the driver 'day ya wust!
Y'filla puss'. A cust an' cust,
'Ya bustad driver day ya wust!'
Um oot the buss! A beet tha dust! A thunk a brork ma fookin' rust.
Ull tullya thus! Ull tullya thus . . .

I toddle haim wi ma disgust. Disgust thuts paled aporn disgust
Ach but no, thuts no the wust.
Thuts no the wust.
There's nay mair trust – aye thuts tha wust
Tha lussies . . . Ach!
An noo a wushed – a wust nay pust – becuss . . .

We kusd!

MIKE MCKEVER

REQUIEM

I heard a crash of thunder, that blew my mind asunder,
A voice called out my number on the last day of my life.
Lightning pierced my vision, images in collision
That danced in wild derision on the shadows of my life.
I smelled the stench of hatred, as bombs blast clouds abated
That turned my lungs to paper, one September of my life.
Glass splintered all around me, girders crushed and bound me.
Timbers warped and bound me and bled me of my life.
Warm blood oozed and soaked me, dust clouds cloaked and choked me
Screams of terror haunted me in the nightmare that was my life.
I didn't kiss my lover, I didn't hug my brother,
I didn't thank my parents for their precious gift of life.
I pray for peace in this land, I pray for peace in their land.
I place myself in God's hand to guide me through the night.
And when it dawns tomorrow, there'll be no grief or sorrow
But empty skies, rusty shells, requiem and Bach.

HAYES TURNER

BISCUIT TINS

Grandma had a biscuit tin
Old and round, colours worn thin.
Inside were treasures from long ago
When much younger she used to sew
There were buckles and buttons by the score
I played with them on the floor
Brass studs from coats and sleeves
Wooden shapes with painted leaves
Tiny ones from baby clothes
Black and navy – lots of those
Pretty glass, pearlies too
Fancy shapes a delicate hue
I liked the buckles too
Bold and shiny – still looked new
Soldiers buckles had a crest
But nurses had the best
Small ones were neat and square
The blue buckles were a pair
All the buckles and buttons told a story
Once when new were in their glory
Grandma's old biscuit tin
Really did have treasures in!

SHEILA WALLER

PURE MATHS

If energy is mass at light speed squared,
Then mass is energy – does this mean ought?
By this equation is the mystery bared?
Or revelation to the spirit brought?
By intellect unaided can we find
A key to open doors in the arcane?
Can written symbols the great scroll unwind?
Or mathematics probe the font of pain?

Pure mathematics is to abstract thought,
As stick to a blind man, it gives him aid,
But cannot give him sight. Its symbols fraught
With meaning only prove that truth essayed
By intellect alone is recondite –
'Tis intuition gives the spirit sight.

HENRY HARDING ROGERS

WAITING

Waiting on a train platform for the last time
grinding teeth, sweat in palms, racing time,

pacing with my hands behind my back, like Dad did
outside the front door, with nails bitten by time.

My father hated waiting. He traced it back to his mother
waiting for his father's homecoming, praying to the God of time.

She waited with nothing but a ration book,
cold pillow, and a clock recalcitrant to time.

He grew up with the sound of ticking clocks,
waiting for bombs to drop, or not drop, hating time.

Now I stand on packed platforms, chewing face
on another granite morning, sweating over time.

Train late by two minutes, iron clamp grips my chest,
my teeth grind, I can't wait, I run to accelerate time.

My father waited for most of his life, in cold sweat
with feet tapping outside the front door, all the time.

When his feet stopped tapping, he closed the door
finally realising waiting is merely watching time.

SOPHIE FENELLA

SOULMATES

You wore,
far too much.
What were you trying to hide?

Secret marks,
beauty spots,
tattoos expressing whom you are inside?

Please confide,
I can feel the fear
reflecting from your burning eyes.

Do not worry.
I will not run to the hills
or burst into flame.

Take off at least one item of clothing.
By telling me your name,
the city you grew up in, even hobbies or dreams.

I may have asked too much too quickly,
judging by your cold enthusiasm.
But how else did you expect me to be,
when my heart wanted to know everything.

Eventually like a tide, your guard came down . . .

Your silk scarf unravelled,
muttering vague answers.
Showing a glimpse of the half-empty cup
of your tiring existence.

Your blue blouse started to unbutton,
keeping me in suspense.
You kept claiming you're not interesting
but that doesn't make sense.

The scar, underneath your velvet bra
was a clear indication of a story untold.
So quit implying that you are unworthy
and tell me that story until it gets old.

More clothing fell during the age of conversation.
I got a great visualisation
of the beauty in your soul,
when you explained all of your hard written history
and why you felt so incomplete.

Tears were shed and knees became weak.
I find it hard to believe that such a lovely person
came from such a disturbing background.

I immediately fell for your being.
Seeing things from your point of view,
like second-hand smoke. We shared the pollution.

I reached to support you,
like the brown belt that was around your waist.
I felt it unbuckle as I released to look back at your face.

More secrets and dreams then became exposed.
That was the moment I saw you completely naked.

It was your decision to let me in and I am glad you did.
Now in my life, you will always remain.
Not as a dirty stain but something more positively, permanently
engraved.

We became more than friends that day,
We became soulmates.

SHELDON SINNAMON

POETRY IN MOTION

A poem committed suicide,
No one to read the words inside,
Her dusty jacket faded grey,
She waited silently every day,
For someone to love and hold her tight,
Someone whose joy she would excite,
Written within were prose and verse,
Other worlds you could transverse,
Alas alack nobody came,
Imagine her feeling of horror and shame,
She threw herself into the fire,
Her dying embers left to inspire.

CHERRY COBB

WONDROUS LOVE

Our love is as solid as the ancient rocks Stonehenge,
Strong and as long as the Golden Gate Bridge Extends.
Romantic as the sparkling Aurora Borealis lights,
The Hanging Gardens of Babylon, held tight like stalactites.

Our love can move Everest, make the Pisa Tower lean,
Spiritual and earnest, as Jerusalem's serene,
Occasionally a fight in Rome's Colosseum,
Woeful regrets laid bare in Tutankhamen's museum.

Our love is impenetrable like the Great Wall of China,
Shiny like the Pyramids, there is nothing finer.
Deserving of a shrine at the foot of Temple Artemis,
Polar Ice caps melt into a soft ambient mist.

Our love is higher than the Empire State can tower,
A jewel within the crown of the Taj Mahal's power,
Colourful as the Barrier Reef, the love we feel inside,
Grander than the Canyon and deeper than it is wide.

CHRISTINE BURROWS

WE WERE ONLY CHILDREN

I was only 16, I was young, I was only a child,
My mothers girl, someone's daughter.
We were only children, convinced it was love.
Convinced we would grow old together, Convinced that we were the
future. That we could change things.
We wrapped ourselves up in a haze of conviction,
Wrapped up in the love, the lust, the late nights, camping out, drinking,
smoking having fun.
Blind to the realism, of the responsibility of how we were supposed to
be.
Ignorant of our actions and the future we were fated to.
Admiration clouded the view of our relationship,darkened my view of
you, of the way things changed, the path we walked and the road we
stumbled.
I looked up to you, you nourished me, sharing trinkets of information,
about science and astronomy, you believed in the things that I did not
understand.
You took me under your wing, tried to teach me of the things you knew,
imparting your knowledge, sowing the seeds, ready for the change in
seasons.
I was only a child when I let you hit me,
When I let you control me.
We were only children, playing at being grown-up.
Trying to live and build our future.
The pressure too much
It broke you, unable to withstand the weight they put on you,
Your shoulders hunched, your knees bent,
You could hardly lift your head.
I tried to carry you, to lift the weight, to help you,
To protect you.
Our love should have been stronger, we should have been invincible,
that bubble never protected us,
Instead it suffocated me, I was the one to blame, it was my fault that you
were weak.
That you could not breathe.
I was the one that made you sick, that panicked you in the middle of the
night, which stopped you from sleeping.

Suicidal thoughts buried themselves in your mind and body, they left you itching, scratching to find the person that was there before, before the blood and the tears and the shame.

I still loved you, in my eyes I needed to make you better, to find that innocent person that loved me when we were only 16.

When we were only children.

When we were naïve to the world and the way we had to be, when we could stay up late and walk for hours.

I didn't want to learn to have to hide the knives, so that you didn't try to attack me.

I didn't want to have to be the one that counted the pills to see how many you had taken.

I wasn't the bad guy, I rang 999, I rang your mum.

You were someone's son, you were someone's lover.

I didn't want you to die, I left it too late, a part of you died that night.

A part of me died too.

I was no longer a child when I realised it was wrong.

That this isn't the way love should be.

You are the reason I have the scars, the reason I fear myself, the darkness that shadows me, these memories imprison me.

You are the reason I taint love with a brush that will never be clean, I offer a broken soul to the world.

Who will take this puppet on his string, who will fix and mend me?

Who will be the patient giver that will care?

In a cold world were people pass you and enjoy the entertainment of the mask you provide.

In a world where people are too busy to stop and watch the world and the people in it.

Is this just another stage, are we all actors, merely playing at being alive?

Am I just another puppet on someone's strings, waiting to be moved and placed in a new scene?

I don't want these strings, I want my Geppetto.

GEMMA PERROTT

BARBIE DOLL

It's scary these days what girls will do to become thinner;
drown in protein shakes, eat nothing but Vogue for dinner.
Why is the ideal woman seen as thin?
When bones visible through clingfilm-like skin
is not my idea of healthy.
You can have a size zero waist but have a size zero brain.
I'm not saying that when you gain
weight you gain intelligence,
I'm saying that when you preach hate and don't appreciate
that weight bears no relevance
then you're not going to get very far.
So don't let a number on a label label who you are.
It's bizarre, that girls starve their confidence, let alone their body,
because small-minded people have bullying as a hobby.
So this one's for the girls who cry in front of the mirror
when the only thing that's cracked is their mentality.
This one's for the girls who dream of being serene when in reality
they're beautiful. Inside and out.
Without the need to pout or throw their fake features about.
I'm not trying to be sarcastic
but I'd rather be genuine than plastic
because Barbie dolls get pulled apart.
What makes a truly strong woman is what's in her heart.
For a start,
you can change weight, complexion, features you wish to hide
but one thing stays constant and that's what's inside.

EVA CURLESS

IN TWISTED RAINBOWS

Pop art biceps
Technicolour triceps
Skittles smile up the arm
Drug-addled
Tantalising
Awash with psychedelic charm

Their broad grins are from a better day
On a tattoo so carelessly tucked away
A polo shirt can barely hide
Where Smarties and shoulder subdivide

Cheeky faces peek through swirling hoops
Block colours blend in florid loops
A living acid trip
Upon a limb
Garishly printed upon a whim
In five shades of carefree

Sketches of spontaneity
A brand of a younger you,
Me, him, her, who
A younger Brigh-tone
The tattoo that is a thousand faces
In twisted rainbows.

GRACE JACKSON

THE ELDERLY COUPLE

The elderly couple hand in hand
Tap their feet to the beat of the band
She looks across . . . a sideways glance
He understands . . . she wants to dance
They move to the beat of the band

He looks good in his crisp new shirt
She leans in closer . . . whispers . . . flirts
In response he strokes her hair . . .
Wonders about her underwear
They have no need for words

They share a smile, a gentle touch
Occasionally their lips may brush
An eyebrow raised, she knows the signs
He's wondering if she feels inclined?
She indicates – no need to rush

It's 4 o'clock in the afternoon
And the tea dance will be ending soon
He holds her close
For the final waltz
Of their second honeymoon

Arm in arm they head for the station
Giggling with anticipation
On arrival home
They unplug the phone
To aid their concentration

Hungrily the pair embrace
Kick back furniture to gain some place
And . . . rehearse the steps they learned today
Practising the art of the swing and sway
They move with style and grace

Sipping cocoa they reminisce
Wondering how it's come to this?
The elderly couple side by side
Sex replaced by the Polly Glide
And the obligatory goodnight kiss.

CATHERINE SCOTT

I AM A MAN

I am a man
I don't need to man up
Because I am already man enough
Whether I'm gay, straight, camp, asexual, metrosexual or utterly
contextual
I am a man

I am a man
I don't need to grow a pair
I already have two balls and a penis
Whether it's an inch, a foot or as big as Mars or Venus
I am a man

I am a man
I don't need any more money than I currently have
It won't make me any more devoted to you than I already am
Nor will it make my heart ache less
At the thought of losing you
Yes I have a heart and I feel and I cry and still
I am a man

I am a man
I don't need to be stronger than your ex
Or better looking than Posh's Becks
I don't need to be as popular as Kanye West
Or have pecs that bulge out of my skin-tight vest
When I don't meet your expectations
Of what Hollywood or the Daily Mail
Tells you a man should be
Don't tell me to 'be a man'
Because I already am

Even if I had no legs
And you had to wheel me around in a chair
With people staring at me here and there
As you feed me
Because I could not feed myself
It would be tough
But I would still be man enough

I am a man
I'm allowed to cry
I'm allowed to be strong
Vulnerable, confused
I'm allowed to be wrong
If I don't know I'm allowed to ask
And I have absolutely no problem multi-tasking

What if you as a woman are the same as me?
With the same fucking ridiculous insecurities
As the rest of the population
Needing self-esteem and validation
What if apart from my penis and your vagina
We are the same with different names
Underneath the skin we're both living in
What if we are both as mindless, anxious and nutty
As each other?
You wanting security inside
Me wanting a good mother for my child
What if we don't need to understand each other?
What if all we need is to accept each other
Tenderly love, communicate and hold each other
Even when you think I'm being a twat
And aiming at my balls with my own cricket bat

What if all we need is each other?
Because no matter what, who, how or why you are
I love and accept you with all your flaws and foibles
From now until you lose your marbles because
You are a woman
And I
I am a man.

PAUL BAICHOO

THE BEAST

When it came to partying, no one could
outlast the beast. It destroyed everything
in its path. A genuine weapon of
mass destruction. Champagne, Drambuie, scotch,
the chosen drink obliterated in
a matter of seconds, forget minutes.

Beast gave us pleasure, beast urged us on to
do whatever we wanted. It was said
that excess was the new norm. And who would
deny the beast? Clearly not you or I.
Complicated, dangerous, sexy – we
all craved a piece of the beast. It was true
our conscience didn't operate in the
party zone. We all looked the other way.

And so it carried on. We kept drinking.
Double vision became triple vision,
double vision became triple vision,
became triple vision.
The beast egged us on, we were mesmerised
by those bubbles. So many rose to the
top but it's the filth that creates the bubbles.
The beast got crazier, drunker, stronger.
We accepted collateral damage
over time – this was another new norm.

As chaos descended over us all
we finally changed but the beast didn't.
You had to admire the beast. The sheer
audacity of the creature to go
on and on, not once looking back to see
the damage caused. It couldn't help itself,
it was born that way and the proud parents
didn't want to be told that there might be
another way. And in all honesty
the beast was too large – too big to jail.

Beast became the hair of the dog and more.
Whenever the hangover lifted and we looked
closely, despairingly, subduedly in
the mirror – there the beast returned our stare.

GAVIN SIMPSON

ANOTHER TOWN

In the early morning
Memories like a lance piercing flesh.
Collective years spent building up,
But the swift tearing down.
Then two years on,
All legal now,
Signed away in ink on a line
And unhappy people left behind.
Someone lay sleeping
While another lay thinking.

Lost in thoughts and kaleidoscope dreams
The comfortable old familiar scenes.
Unregistered recent and present events,
In the mind the old life still presents.

In dreams some lovely golden day
With summer's colours
Fragrance
Sounds,
And games of tennis on the grass.
Children's laughter
Fun and love,
At a table with an umbrella
Eating meals outside together . . .

A cold breeze blows
A sudden chill
Grey clouds throng up
A vision fades.
The need to reach and touch someone
But turning round to find them gone

In the bedroom's dimness of divided belongings,
Looking down on the street,
At trees
And tall white buildings.
Eyes fixed on a point directly opposite
Where the car was parked a long time ago
In happiness, contentment and innocence.

And beyond the streets and amusement arcades
The grey heaving sea pounds waves on the shore
Of another seaside resort.

CHRISTINE ANN MOORE

RAPPING GRANNY

I'm going to be a rapper but they say I'm too old
Now that mean comment leaves me stone-cold.
I've got the rhythm and I've got the beat
From my blue rinsed hair right down to my arthritic feet.
The toe tapping with gout's no fun
But for rap rap rapping it's got to be done.
And other than that I'm well equipped
Because thanks to surgery I've been re-hipped.
They say that I'm from the wrong generation
But I've got plenty of inspiration
From the many pop idols of my distant past
So pin back your ears and I'll give you a blast.
I've written a poem that'll give you a clue
And when I've finished you can tell me who

I rock and roll and I twist and shout
I swivel my hips and let it all hang out
In my drain pipe trousers and my blue suede shoes
And my lame tuxedo I can sing the blues
The girls all scream when I start to sing
Because I'm a Hound Dog and I'm The King.

Now don't tell me that you don't recognise
That owner of those shaking thighs
That champion of the rotating pelvis
You've got it in one
His name is . . . Elvis!

I went to the cavern where the Beatles were live
And man oh man, you should have seen me jive.
With my beehive hair do and a beam on my face
My partners threw me all over the place
In my circular skirt like a whirling dervish
My arms just giving that additional flourish
We oldies keep these good memories alive
As that is the means by which we thrive.
Forget the bad ones, they'll do you no good
And just put you into a grumpy mood.

I love this rapping now I'm in the groove,
It's the perfect therapy for making you move.
But now I've started I just can't stop
So I'll have to keep going until I drop

Down

Dead.

JULIET BORLAND

WONDERLAND

From the crevice of my eye I saw
A frog land in a cup of dew . . .
A pouch of emerald leather,
He was frantic to escape.
Stranded in his mini oxbow lake,
I scooped him gently from the slurry soup
And felt his heart flick,
Ticking fast against my palm.
I lost him for a while
When he hopped into the grass
And I went back to poking pinks in pots –
Re-surfacing, he leapt into the air,
Startling the bare bones out of me
And what I saw was straight from Wonderland –
Alice would have been at home all right,
A butterfly was riding on his head –
A cabbage white, fluttering
To keep his balance straight.
I'll never see the like of that again –
A way out craziness that made my day.
You could say – a phenomenon.

JENNIFER D WOOTTON

THE OLIVE HARVEST

It was mid-September. We each recall times
unlike this – with square locked fists, lakes for
eyes like waterfalls from an abyss. Zionists burn
olive trees again. We endure each remain.

The sun and soil wake.

Palestinians are snowflakes falling on blushing
cheeks and blood is an inconvenient thing;
staining this Palestinian stain; soiling Israeli soil.
Olives are bled for a price – unlike us.

Mother cries delirious; brother crushes olives.
Desperate tears strike a hot knife; simmering
heart coals reach for my son – stolen. Soldiers
spit flames seething. Farmers douse olive trees.

The sky and trees sleep.

Octobers first day falls to gaunt shapes like
our harvest, our orchard and our homeland.
Trees are silent when you burn them. Olives

are still when you bleed them – unlike me.

PAUL POINT

MAN WITH GOLD
(NO SORROW IN HIS HEART)

Floating on peaceful waters
he collects the gold from the sea
places it in his boat
feeding his addiction.

His hair grows from where he has not slept for long
his face dry and disorientated
slowly he unfolds the tale of how he the master of all gold
stole the hearts of the gold.

He tells his wandering children of the mountains
how he promises to give them all the gold in the world
and makes an empire of all things valuable and bright.

The next thing he knows he sees diamonds fall from the sky
slowly mesmerised from staring too long makes him go blind.
All the visions he sees are silver and gold
with gold in his heart

his soul bitter and old
his heart no feeling but gold

until one day when he lay to rest
and one of his children became unwell

he tried to save her by feeding her gold
but the shore witnessed this with eyes to
pry and gave him nothing but a choice to make

gold or his child.

With the dilemma in mind he chose to water the sky
and take out a star where he would place it in her heart

so on his journey of discovery he fed his child the star
and she became better

now the shore released him from the hallowing waters
and gave him the strength to say gold is not everything

and gold cannot buy you health or happiness.

So now the shore can rest and
the man who once thought gold was everything
can rest assured and live happily with his children
with love and not gold no more.

LEANNE DRAIN

A FINE DRIZZLE VEILS

Whatever light the sun might vow –
raincoat grey and grubby flannel
clouds turn up then anyhow,
to ooze and seep far from a channel.

It's August – summer will turn to go,
weeping sodden rose petals,
visiting birds somehow know –
every cooling breeze unsettles

then in nests. Soon they assemble
on telegraph wires, discussing when
to depart, their youngsters tremble.
Such is Nature's regimen.

GILLIAN FISHER

DEFINE

Do not define me as a little girl who always cries
For I am a girl that tries and tries
Until she dies to work hard for what she believes in

Do not confine me within your narrow, 2D way of thinking
That I am just a little brown girl
Not worthy to make a difference

Do not define me by the strange cotton clothes I wear
Or the shades of mehendi in my hair
I am much more than my foreign appearance

Do not define me by the brown colour of my skin
And assume the culture I am in
Is too alien to consider me a friend

Do not define me by the language that I speak
And disregard its unique
By saying you're weak with laughter when you hear it

Do not define me the god that I believe in
And say your people are the reason
This world has lost its peace and cohesion

I will not be defined.

ZENIB AKHTAR

THE TEMPEST

A fierce soul sings its tale to me

Enraged in its chains, it demands to be free.
In a moment he unveils the pain he hid away,
The way they would hurt him, like a predator upon his prey.

His painful opera fills me with sympathy,

Years of discomfort has now left him empty.
The screams of anger come pouring out,
Now who he can trust remains as a doubt . . .

His high-pitched cries are invading my sleep,

The sounds of his pain are ever so deep.
His story is able to move even the hardest of hearts,
Snatch away your peace and make you fall apart.

Just like a tempest he is outraged,
From all this agony he feels caged.
So far from love he suffers within,
To distract him from this, he continues to sing.

After releasing himself from this misery,
He is now able to breathe peacefully.
After a calming end comes along a sigh of relief,
As he executes from his life this sense of grief.

SANNA AKRAM

GOREE

I walked on your golden sand
And felt the warmth of the African sun
And my heart bled.
I saw the sunlight on the azure sea
Reflecting the blueness of the sky
And hung my head.
For this is my island in the sun
My ancestry – and yet
There is a sadness.
Beneath the sand I feel the pain
Invisible blood trickling through my toes
I can't forget.
The cruel oppression of your slavery
Chains and cold damp prison walls
Steeped in human tears.
Your sand should be blood-red
Lapped by black seas of despair
And yet – I proudly lift my head, and smile
To be a part, however small, of this
For we are survivors, standing tall
Sparkling in the sunshine,
And you will always be – my island in the sun
Rising above the misery.

LILIAN FULKER

SESTINA SELF-REFLECTION

As I spray and rub the hardened spots
they start to fade, and the face in glass,
a crucible of creases, reveals age
I rarely see when peering at this man
whose face stares back at me with cruelty.
His air is that of one who has the right

to shock me in this way, convinced that he is right.
All these unseeing years I've failed to spot
time's marks that have accrued cruelly,
or have I seen but scorned the glass'
evidence, convinced this mortal man
is merely maturing with this thing called age?

It is a feature of this fussy age
that people no longer have the right
to wither naturally, so modern man
resorts to beauty aids that veil the spot,
the blemish, which offends the looking glass
and quantifies the years so cruelly.

What seems still crasser and more cruel
is that for years I've misconstrued my age,
ignoring what is truly in the glass,
not seeing my farewell to youth aright,
and thinking I'm forever young, a spot
of self-deceit which bolsters mirror man.

I mind a time long gone when this child-man's
reflection was another mite – such cruel
deceit, quite discrete; this wicked spot
in time, the consciousness of which does age
me as I study left side and the right,
is imprisoned in the twisting glass.

Is this soul I see now in candid glass
that being from the past, that man,
or the myself of now, the husband right,
the caring father, grandad with cruelly
wrinkled skin, denoting tired age
and timeworn air not difficult to spot.

Illumined on the spot I stroke the glass,
which truly shows a man his actual age;
it is not cruel, I see, but simply right.

WES ASHWELL

THE VANQUISHED LION

The covenant that I entered
In recent years has been betrayed
And yet still I walk with tired grace
Though I am bred for desolation
At their shoulder but ill-ventured
I saw your enemies allayed
But without contrition in your face
For sacrifice in name of nation

For the asking I would labour
To take brave young men and build them
Should you have reason to be frightened
They promised gallantry and shields
You forced their virtue and sabre
Through the lives of foreign children
Your highbrow claim to be enlightened
In trading poppy for oil fields

For the needless death of soldiers
What corner of ancient London
Must we fill with all your naked shame
Yet keep the honour she encloses
For the coat that drapes my shoulders
Once reflecting valour golden
Is now a blood-dried matted mane
Of faded wilten Tudor roses

I still carry Nelson's guile
Wolfe's compassion is not deceased
I know the enemy's widow grieves
When the night reveals my rifle trace
How will I feel in my last mile
Before I sleep will I find peace
In the shadow of England's leaves
I hope to slip this blessed place

But should I hear the same bell toll
If I am asked to play my part
I will take up arms roaring aloud
And step once more into the breach
With soiled lungs and a clean soul
Worn out claws and a scarred heart
On a broken path but fighting proud
With truth in sight but out of reach.

GALAHAD JONES

AN OLD MAN WEEPS

An old man on a hillside weeping
Sees the valley quietly weeping
Sees the rivers overgrown
Hears the melancholy song
Of a lone corncrake
No more singing in the valley
The joy of people toiling together
All has changed, homes stately grand
Gon's the thatched cottage with few acres of land
That sustained the family
That's why on a hillside an old man weeps
He thinks of times that used to be
Warmth and love of a family
Ruins of his humble home
Presents the happiness he has known
That's why on a hillside an old man weeps
He sees a country darkened with despair
Waiting for the day that will carry his breath away
Over there where he will rest in peace, perfect peace.
That's why on a hillside
An old man weeps.

FRANCES GIBSON

COFFEE

Shut your belated breath,
your 'this isn't coffee' mouth
and open your eyes to see the black pond staring right at you,
open your nostrils and smell the overpowering caffeine
and say it one more time.
'This isn't coffee'
are your nose hairs failing you?
Are you living in a parallel universe where this is the ceiling and that's the
floor?
Or did I just black out and imagine putting coffee in this mug?
And sure that mug is a bit small, but I couldn't find one bigger than you!
Are you going to tell me that's not a chair?
Because that's in front of me too.
And this smile isn't genuine.
This smile wants to punch you.
This smile wants to spill coffee – that's right, coffee,
over that distasteful jumper.
But the manager's watching
and this smile needs that 6.50 an hour.
So maybe if I put a fourth teaspoon in you might,
taste its prominent coffee characteristics and,
come to the conclusion it's not tea!

CHARLOTTE SOUTER

MAGIC PINS

The doctor kept sticking it in
her wrist
I try not to get pissed off
but my thoughts are in the grip of
the knife's thrust and twist
as needle after needle gives her a long kiss
each smooch a bout of pain as it tries to lick a vein
its lipstick stains spotty bruised train tracks
purple and splotched the doctor feigns there's a knack
he feigns there's a knack, it's about the angle
it's about the force, it's about the depth
it's about the depths you'll plumb
just to stop her being the first one.
(That you lose)

The doctor kept sticking it in,
her arm
I weren't born on a farm
you took an oath to do no harm
if she was awake to say it hurt
would you have another jab at it?
Do you want to make an example
and take another ten samples
you got every faith in the shake
and the quiver of your hand?
Or has your liver turned to lily
as forever drips by
like a morphine feed
or the fluids she needs
your water's wasted on tears
can you biopsy fear?
'Cause you can certainly smell it.

But the doctor kept sticking it in
that thing
that magic pin
making something habitual
from his shrink-wrapped ritual

she's still limp like a string doll
eyes as blank as buttons and still they roll
back into her head heavy as lead
when I get bastard sick I'll ask the undead
oh Baron Samedi won't you take me?
I can't tell between pentagrams and asterisks anymore
in a heartbeat I'd sell my soul for an ambulance
the 999 operator can come later
She wasn't nearly as quick
as the guy on the end of 666.

HARVEY JAMES

THE NEW POET MANIFESTO

One. You a poet. You too have the ghosts of spilled ink from poets past coursing through the fissures in your finger prints. These dints throb and tap to the rhythm of the flint that sparks against your corneas.

Two. Sorry, you can't stop being a poet. You start arguments with your friends over Nicki Minaj's improper use of similes, you edit adverts to get rid of the clichés, you wake up in the middle of the night with rhyming couplets behind your eyes, you pull apart yourself and plunge into the sludge and your muses until you mould the raw dough into palatable stanzas.

Three. Your voice is special, and don't let anybody tell you that it isn't, but poetry is a conversation. Don't forget to read things beside your own work.

Four. Your shed is infinite. Spend your life hanging tools on the walls. You'll use them some day.

Five. Your shell is a myth from the silk of stories you've laced between your bones. It is as beautiful as the sludge it hides, but it does not define you. It's okay to break out of yourself and expose your most vulnerable edges.

Six. Poets are like buffalo. They graze on the savannah with bodies that swallow sunlight and thick horns, but they will welcome strangers to their herd with flapping ears and a playful chuff. All you need to do to join them is join them.

Seven. The most intricately crafted metaphors can be lost in the abyss between mouth and microphone. Be aware of your surroundings. Grab the stand with both hands.

Eight. Don't be bland. Your mind did not pour out hurricanes for your mouth to drought. Spit tsunamis. The audience will ride the wave.

Nine. Play with the rules. But don't be horrified if they don't laugh. Just make sure everyone is aware that you're playing. Nothing is worse than an offensive comment under the guise of post-modernist left-wing double-barrelled poetic irony.

Ten. Breathe. Your poemwasnotwrittenasonewordsodon'treaditasone.

Eleven. There is no money or fame in poetry. You were born two hundred years too late for that.

Twelve. You are a poet. You possess the greatest gift. There is nothing more powerful than immortality.

CHARLEY GENEVER

WE'RE NOTHING ALIKE

You and I – we're nothing alike. Not just because of the ocean between us,
but you in your loud, tie-dye kaftans, twig ankles on show,
and I in muted, grey dresses, leggings all the way to the floor.
You, with your hair crammed into rainbow wraps; my waves flying.

The unhurried bounce in your step, your flip flops beating a rhythm
on your soles; I shuffling discreet on pavements.
Your liquid mocha skin, piercing black eyes and mine sunken,
unquestioning – we're nothing alike.

Your sandpaper palms, mine newborn. Your deep, throaty laugh,
mine held back. Your gestures stretched, mine tamed.
Your fondness for slipping mangoes through your teeth
on yawning afternoons; mine for spending – we're nothing alike.

Your detours on the way home from school for fried cassava
at roadside stalls; mine for Ben and Jerry's Cookie Dough.
Your easy patience, my fierce lack. Your solitary walks across lowland
plains, come sun, Saharan wind or shower; my rush-hour drives.

You praying for rain to ripen the grain sometimes,
you thanking the clouds for abstaining sometimes; I cursing the sky
for spitting each time – we're nothing alike.

Your shared dreams: I'll study further, Father will stop worrying
about Isaac, Isaac will stop baiting older boys; my dreams
mine: I'll be known, I'll be known.

You, lying outside, making quilts out of stars; I, jerking curtains shut
at the first sign of dark. You, hungry for stories at your grandmother's side,
I kissing mine on the cheek, then retreating upstairs –
we're nothing alike.

And I'll tell myself this, so when head heavies one day,
when your throat grows glass shards in its walls,
when fire tiptoes within you, I'll still sleep at night.

And I'll tell myself this, so when your muscles feel they've been pulped
by a fist, when the ground draws you near,

when your sight starts to mist, I'll still sleep at night.

We're nothing alike, and I'll tell myself this,
so when you're laid on a bed,
when pus bubbles up on your arms and your legs,
when blood inks from your ears, I'll still sleep at night.

And I'll tell myself this, so when your insides collapse
like a jenga tower, when each breath is a mountain climb,
when your brother begins to cry, I'll still sleep at night.

We're nothing alike, and I'll tell myself this,
so when the ebb and flow of your chest starts to slow,
when you're suddenly still, when your mother beats her breast,
when your father's screams shake the earth,
when you're carried out in a black body bag,
I'll still sleep at night.

You and I, we're nothing alike,
we're nothing alike, we're nothing alike.

SHRUTI CHAUHAN

MY ART

My art does so kindly when needed, sedate strong emotion, over feeling,
The sole purpose of it arouses tranquillity and healing,
It lends the mind to a calm and peaceful place,
Away from stirring problems, we so daily face,
My art sweetly makes sense of the convolutions in my head,
It tames and sends to slumber, the monster under my bed,
It affords self-expression, it sets the wind unto my sails,
My art is there to catch me, when my other endeavours fail,
It takes my heart in its grasp, and grants it its desire,
My art is the tiniest flame, and the blazing roaring fire,
It soothes and inspires, it plants the seeds of self-discovery,
And caressing my wounded mind, it granted my recovery,
My art wages civil war, declaring bloody defiance,
It's the shaking of hands in the aftermath, the overdue compliance,
My art leaks into every practice and every action of my own,
It's the furthest distance I've travelled, it's the closest thing to home,
My art is the province in which I stand, dressing me in familiarity,
My art plays common ground, where there breeds great disparity,
My art is the circus, it moves and it arrives,
My art is pure energy, it transforms and never dies,
It finds in me a valiant hero, and comforts the lonely coward,
It's the fleeting seasons that change with the months, the April rains in
which I shower,
My art is the eternal spectrum, colours that splash across my sight
It is the faces of the prism, curious dispersal of white light
My art can be nocturnal, breathing alertness into hours black,
My art is the creased clothes, that after a journey long, you begin to
unpack,
It bites like December winter, it froths like a foamy sea,
My art is the epicentre of my being, the definition of me.
It is the pathways on my palms and the planets in my eyes,
My art is everything that hides among us, so let it choose its best
disguise.

ELIZABETH FRANCES GARNETT

130

6 WEEKS

I see purple and yellow all lined across my streets
Engraved insignias claiming economic feats
I see eyes wide but blinded
Above thin frowns
Chasing my footsteps
Ushering me out the town
I see words of hate
Shrouded by ignorance
Shouted by militants
Embedded and impotent
I see rocks thrown
Blood run into royal blue
The white stained obvious to see but don't forget those eyes are blinded
I see tears moisten fabric
Eyes dark with fatigue
With every insult and threat is it not plain to see?
I see anger
Across both sides
Though I'm sure only few are truly aware of the reasons why
I see hollow shells
And buildings with tall fences
And huddled within are those with dulled pensive
I see cannons of water and bullets of the rubber kind
But they still break your bones
They still damage your mind
I see signs with simple words though the message is clear
Because those signs are symbolic
They emote fear
I see curtains pulled
So that light cannot enter
As sirens pass in search for new dissenters
I see black boots march the streets
Hoods of white tinged with yellow and purple pleats
I see the future across two roads
One shows hope
The other?

ROBERT AWOSUSI

131

THE FEW

Each year these cliffs, protectors of our land,
Like sentinels above the sea they stand,
Play hose again to heroes, gallant few,
Yet fewer now, as time will take its due.

Outside the huts you sat, prepared to fly
And take off in the early morning sky,
To be the first to see Luftwaffe's might,
To play a deadly game by day or night.

Above the green and pleasant land below,
So young, fresh out of school, you fought the foe,
You diced with death each lovely summer's day,
While those you left could only watch and pray.

As vapour trails across the sky you made,
You saw the fields in which you ran and played,
And knowing all the while the cause was just,
You sought no fame, yet fame was on you thrust.

And now with sticks supporting ageing limbs
You stand saluting all with prayers and hymns,
Rememb'ring friends you lost in freedom's fight,
So many years ago, yet mem'ry's bright.

Remember Ginger, by these cliffs shot down,
Brave Jock who pancaked in the sea to drown,
Poor Toby in his cockpit trapped in flame,
Each one they flew to sacrifice and fame.

Deep in a wood sleeps Rob where he came down,
It's said he gave his life to miss the town,
Tim's victory roll turned out to be his last,
He paid the price for landing much too fast.

Now one lone Spitfire flies these cliffs again
With stirring engine note that fires the brain,
It rolls away the years as youth returns,
For one brief fleeting moment passion burns.

These brave and modest men we came to see,
Who fought the good fight that we might be free,
All through the years we will remember you,
So much owed by so many to so few.

PETER ELGAR

TYLER

Tyler lives with his mum
He goes to school where his friends are funny
The carpet in his bedroom's his favourite colour
Blue
His room has stars on the ceiling
He really likes stars
He likes to see the cars outside his window

His mum opens his curtains every morning to wake him up for school
One morning she left them shut
She made beans on toast for him like normal
But they were cold

Another day there was a man in a suit
Tyler thought it was funny that he didn't take his shoes off
Mum only allowed people to come in with their shoes off
But he had a really big folder
So it meant he could stand
Whilst Mum was seated
'Choose which one you'll be in,'

She cried
His shoes clacked as he left
Tyler asked her why
There were houses on their kitchen table

'He wants us to say goodbye
There are richer houses
Richer people
That need to buy
The land we stand on
Make it glass

We have to go
But they'll be far funnier boys
Than the ones in class
This new area will be lovely.
They'll say this house
And all the others
Are broken

They cannot last
So they've bought it and forgotten to ask.'

Tyler didn't want to leave
James and Rohan
His friends on the street
When they'd surf down his stairs
He wants it again and again
He begs to stay
Asks his teacher if he can keep the way
His mum opens his curtains in the morning
The way the stairs look when he's falling downwards
The glint of his stars that shatter his ceiling

This new house didn't have stairs
It had a lift that broke
His mum said they were called 'flat'
The school kids stared at the boy with the hat
With cars on
He sometimes drove past the new houses
They're made of glass
The marble floors sparkle
Maybe, he thought
They used the stars
From his room.

PHOEBE WAGNER

BEST POEM OF A GENERATION

I wish I was one of those
broody, edgy poets
whose writing howls with
unashamed phallocentricity,
living in my city centre flat,
smoking twenty
fags
a day, with my dark-haired lover.

Keruack, Whitman or Ginsberg
would be on my bookshelf,
and we would discuss the metaphysical
nature of the universe.

Perhaps one day my poetry
could be taken to court,
or extracted from the natural curriculum
for its errant cock and balls.

I haven't the attention span.
I'd blame my parents
but I actually quite like them.

STEPHEN FOOT

MAKING

I tried to make something.
My hands know how to make. They are strong.
I thought of the thing, and I brought it to the front of my mind.
When it was there I examined it.

I thought of the shape of it: big as my head.
I thought of the weight of it: bag of flour.
I thought of the feel of it: hard and dull.
I thought of the breath of it: still and seldom.
I thought of the hue of it: soil and yellow.
I thought of the age of it: ancient and new.
I thought of the smell of it: slightly metallic.
I thought of the sound of it: spade hitting bone.
I thought of the taste of it: inedible now.
I thought of the life of it: aeons of stars.
I thought of the sap of it: splintered away.
I thought of the love of it: face turned up.
I thought of the count of it: alone in the world.
I thought of the song of it: brittle and low.
I thought of the heat of it: cool but not cold.
I thought of the thought of it: mourned and missing.
I thought of the space of it: lying in the crook of my left arm.
I thought of the shape of it: roundish, curled in on itself,
With a lip and funnel to an inside that is slippery, smooth and dark.

And I flexed my wide hands, slowly.
I did not know where to start.

RUTH BARKER

BRIAN'S CURSE

Brian sees right through his replacement –
A retired radiologist, finding fractures in this practitioner's practised appearance,
Revealing an as yet unuttered verdict.
A mercilessly easy game for experienced eyes.

To be offered a seat and recognise
The awkward shuffle of shoes,
Professionally sympathetic eyes,
A distinctive hesitation so acutely aware

Of the time it occupies.

To expertly detect these cracks,
And know his diagnosis before it is spoken –
This is his curse.

As anticipation grows, tumour-like in the mind,
He is plagued by one question:
How to break the news,
Without also breaking her?

He imagines a word he has used so many times before
Falling from his soon-still lips, bare and forgiving –

'Terminal'.

And sending tremors rippling through her heart.

His former bride-to-be, now wife,
Had always refused to hear his hospital horror stories –
'What happens in the ward stays there, Brian. Tragedy isn't catching.'

But this,
This,
This diagnosis is
As much hers as his,
And no patient-doctor confidentiality permits
Ignorant bliss –
Safe unawareness
For the widow-to-be.

Brian knows now –
To die happy is to die in the bed of another,
Not shrouded in white cotton belonging to none
Save traces of sickly souls that rested there once –
Lost spirits staining sterile sheets.

His successor makes final preparations
To lose where no success can last.
Two eyes dart desperately across a chart –
A familiar, futile prayer for a mistake.

Our Father, who art in Heaven
Heartless be thy game
Have you no shame?

The throat clears and stabilises,
Delivers the first of its now redundant words:
'Brian-'.

LOLA HOURIHANE

GODDESS

'I hear you like to get with white guys'
He says to me
Oh
Sorry
I'd forgotten
How good of you to remind me that my body is not for me
'Heard? From who?'
That I am not allowed to just be
He shrugs
'Around'
I have never met Around

'Is it true?'
His words are heavy with expectation I cannot carry
Not when my back is already burdened
With trauma untold
What does he want me to say?
We both know that 'no' is a lie
But the truth is a wound that cannot be closed
It doesn't just hurt
It aches
And when the finger of blame is pointed
I will lose that game
And with it, my worth
Because we all know
How the value of property is determined
By its reputation

Why does it matter?
No
Do better
Tell me to –
'Go fuck yourself'
Drink in his response
Like water

He thinks because his hand once stroked the curve of your hips
And his mouth is accustomed to the curve of your lips
That he can bend you to his will
Has he forgotten who you are?
You are a goddess
And he is blessed to be in your presence.

CYNTHIA OTOTE

MIND THE GAP

If you haven't yet heard of the thigh gap
let me quickly fill you in;
it's society's latest weapon
to keep women wafer-thin

or at least give us something to strive for.
Its meaning won't surprise;
if you stand with your feet together
it's the space between your thighs.

What d'you mean there isn't a gap there?
It defines your beauty and worth
in precisely the way that we all know it's fair
to judge every man by his girth.

If you've failed to achieve a thigh gap
shame on you, there is no excuse,
for there's friendly advice all around us
and the womanly wisdom's profuse.

There are blogs on achieving a thigh gap
and I'm sure you would like to learn move
so buy books which go into more detail,
get a gap that all men will adore.

There's a Wiki on gaining a thigh gap
in twenty-six simple steps,
even Twitter accounts owned by thigh gaps;
I'd say that's the weirdest one yet.

They advise . . .

squatting and lunging
with cardio exercise,
rubbing old coffee grinds
onto your limbs,
counting the calories,
cutting out alcohol,
all in pursuit of a
fine pair of pins.

And you should . . .

exercise daily,
avoid over-eating,
make sure that you body brush
three times each week,
wear thigh-slimming shapewear
to tone down your lady lumps
all for the sake of
that perfect physique.

You must use . . .

creams to eradicate
dimples and cellulite,
pants that pull in for a
slim silhouette.
Can't afford surgery?
Take out a loan,
an investment that surely
you'll never regret.

So find your . . .

own thinspiration
in Pinterest pin-ups
to lay off the puddings
and stay on those scales
for we all know it's never
our spirit or mind
but the size of our thigh gap
which interests males.

Now, it's hardly a novel concept
that females are judged by their size
but it seems women's worth is now rated
on the space between their thighs.

which for many will always be zero
if their hips are too close set;
their genetics might prevent it
no matter how skinny they get.

By all means eat less junk food,
limit sugar and trans-fats and salt
but if you are troubled or lonely
it isn't your thigh gap's fault.

And it's women who help this myth flourish,
so we stress and obsess on our legs,
but how is a girl meant to blossom
when she's pining for Barbie doll pegs?

So I say . . .

no to their diets,
their nipped and tucked torsos,
their tanners and bronzers
which shadow and shape,
their Photoshopped lifestyles,
their detox then re-tox,
I'd rather be me-sized
than shaped like a rake.
I won't join a gym
or hire personal trainers,
I've far more fun methods
of spending my pay,
I spit on the website that
airbrushes teens
and refuse to do
twenty plus butt lifts a day.

I will not run my life
based on fasting and fainting
egged on by a model
who's built like a stick
and whose digitised bodies
held up as a grail.
Their binging and purging
advice makes me sick.

But I realise I offered my wisdom,
said I'd teach you those two quick steps,
so if you still long for a thigh gap

make sure that you don't forget

that your worth can be seen in your body
in the space between your thighs.
Dissent or disagree and you'll be
soon cut down to size.

Top tips for achieving a thigh gap?
My wisdom I'll now impart:
just eat what you need to be healthy
and stand with your feet apart.

AMY RAINBOW

STIRLING TO GLASGOW

A hollow can,
Containing souls,
Each one different,
Never whole.

Look on down?
They all do.
Do not speak.
Why won't you?

This strange place
Empty eyes.
Leave no trace,
Speak white lies.

They tell tales,
I can tell.
Some have joy –
Others Hell.

I shall move.
I shall speak.
They do not –
The blessed meek.

We are weary.
In these lights.
Let this bullet,
Shoot through night.

CATHERINE CHRISTIE

DESPAIR

In the depths of despair she lays
Her every waking moment is a grim reminder of her reality
Dusk turns to dawn
And time stands still yet again
In the awkward stillness of her mind
Pieces of her fragmented life begin to piece together
The overwhelming feeling of no control floods her soul
Engulfing her consciousness with a torrent of abuse
Irrigated tears fall from her face
This existence is tearing her apart
Turning a once-compassionate heart to stone
But yet again life continues around her
She is isolated by her own bitterness
Precious moments evade her
Time she'll never get back escape her
This reflection demands her to analyse the past
In a desperate bid to realise where it all went wrong
Questions emerge, premonitions of a stagnant future appear and doubt
rears its ugly head
Why is this happening to her?
And why does it seem so out of control
If she acts to try and make a change what will be the repercussions of
her decision
Is she really ready to face that dilemma?
Again time stands still
As if to say the thoughts aren't worth having
And again all is calm in the domains of her turbulent mind
Her anger has subsided and her temper is subdued
Till the next episode of the inevitable
Her life remains at a standstill.

PATRICIA STEIN-WOOLDRIDGE

147

ALL WRONG

I'm all wrong today
in the way
that my telly volume is too high
or too low and I don't know why.
It's broken in a similar vein
to the wrong way it didn't rain
today. The sun was wrongly shining
and forgot what season it was defining.
The faded, the jaded yellow sun rises
on another day full of promise of sweet sad surprises.
In Shakespeare the characters had their rain
and their storms to match their pain
I have not even that. It's all wrong
and I have nowhere that I belong.

People die and cry and lie
and grieve for the dead.
Cameron with his shiny head
so shiny, like it's been painted
over his thoughts, tainted
with the feinted glory of war
and I don't know what for.

I know that people die and cry
and all tell a monstrous lie
when we say that we know
what's happening, because we show
that we don't by living our lives
in tiny beehives
buzzing in and out making honey
and bowing down to the great god, money
and oil and whatever it is that makes them piss
their pants with bliss because we go buzz
and they move us
whichever way they want.

Who are 'they'?
They are you and they are me
and everything they want us to be
and it is me, because in Cameron's eyes
and Blair's lies, it's me and it's you
we have the blood of it through
us and in us and it is us
Buzz, buzz

Can you hear the cries, the lies?
Bodies exploded and dreams imploded
in Baghdad's dead, and Beirut had bled
and Lebanon cries for the body of lies
that kills people in Paris but not only there
in every gritty city, there is pity
for what we have become
but let us be numb
and bomb the fuck out of Syria
in senseless hysteria.

Is the colour of our blood not red?
Does it matter the skin we are in
if we're dead?
No more.
No more fucking war.

Can you hear the pain, the cries?
Do you want all the puzzled hurt to rise?
Swamp you, drown you, pull you under?
Now it should rain and now it should thunder
with a people riding with one voice
to say no, this is not my choice.
This is so badly wrong
and it cannot belong
in us.

We must not buzz, we must rise above lies
and truly see that 'they'
are you and 'they' are me
I believe in a different way to be.

I don't believe I am so wrong
because I am you and we belong
to a new day and a different way
and a new generation of 'they'.

KIMBERLEY MARTINEZ

THE TERMINUS

It is with a dust-shod shade of grey,
that I leave the terminus late of day.
A weak filtered light flickers then dies,
plunging to shadow the blue of the sky.

For this is a town with nowhere to go,
where hope and ambition expands and flows
through the hub of a pricey all-girl's school,
with the private use of a swimming pool.

For this is a town fed on cheap fast food
and the shady thrills of the gambling hall,
where even estate agents sit and brood
as their pictures glare out shabby and small.

It's as if hope died at the end of the line,
where even the stones of the old church pine,
and shocked at the greying suburban sprawl,
send headstones tumbling to the bearing wall.

Then askew and ragged like old men's teeth,
standing sentinel to the path beneath,
roses thrust fecundity, pinks and reds,
from the richest loam of embodied beds.

Then office girls saunter with skirts cut high,
and chattering voices – unseeing eye,
they think amorous thoughts of love and men
and how tonight, they may love once again.

RICK TAYLOR

INDEX

Names in bold indicate Slam Finalists

FORWARD POETRY
INFORMATION

We hope you have enjoyed reading this book - and that you will continue to enjoy it in the coming years.

If you like reading and writing poetry drop us a line, or give us a call, and we'll send you a free information pack.

Alternatively if you would like to order further copies of this book or any of our other titles, then please give us a call or log onto our website at www.forwardpoetry.co.uk

Forward Poetry Information
Remus House
Coltsfoot Drive
Peterborough
PE2 9BF
(01733) 890099